Reminiscences of a Travelling Vet

Charles Frank

Romney Publications

Published by

Romney Publications
351 Exning Road · Newmarket · Suffolk CB8 0AU

First published 1999

Designed and Typeset by
Equine Veterinary Journal Ltd

Printed by
Geerings of Ashford · Ashford · Kent · England

Cover illustration by:
Graham Fowell "The Hit Man"

Contents

Introduction

Practice life for a vet means that you are continually busy, rushing from one appointment to another and always at least half an hour later than intended. Clients, especially racehorse trainers, are governed by numerous claims on their time and are thus disinclined to be kept waiting. Strangely this does not occur to them when you have seen the two horses for which you were summoned. They then happily suggest that there are another three animals which they would wish you to see. This means that your tight schedule has once again gone for the proverbial Burton and stress is then the master.

For this reason a call which meant travelling beyond the practice perimeter always sounded welcome. The following tales go some way to explain that further pastures were not always as rosy as optimistic hopes had built. After nearly thirty years at the daily grind of practice, I felt that there could be other fields of endeavour which might not be so demanding. As a result I left the practice and embarked on the life of a consultant. This gave me great thoughts of importance. Thoughts that were to wilt like flowers in the desert when I discovered that twenty four hours covered the average memory span of the majority of my old clients.

As has been said many times, fate has frequent surprises in store for the unsuspecting. My experience was to be in demand, although in pastures far from those I had expected.

A brief but enjoyable career as a bloodstock agent brought a number of challenging visits to various horse sales around the world. Alas, I soon found out that my metier was not to be found in persuading prospective owners that a particular horse was their heaven-sent passport to racecourse glory and riches. Years of viewing the many vicissitudes which can afflict a horse lead me to believe that no animal, however prepossessing it seemed in the sale ring, was likely to be able to avoid at least one of the crippling unsoundnesses which are common to the horse. The immortal words of Jorrocks kept ringing in my ears:

Introduction

"What warrant him sound! I would not even warrant him to be a horse!"

Shortly before realism brought my bloodstock days to an end, I was proposed as the British representative on the veterinary committee of the International Equestrian Federation (FEI). This, the body which controls equestrian sports such as show jumping, eventing, dressage and driving, opened fresh doors for me. Annual visits to headquarters in Switzerland for committee meetings under the auspices of a charming Russian professor, who spoke no more than a sprinkling of English, were interspersed by forays to equine competitions in many varied parts of the world. These culminated in the Olympic Games in Korea, of which more later.

Once more fate intervened when I was asked to act as an expert witness in a High Court case in London. This lead on to my becoming an integral member of the Veterinary Defence Society, which dealt with a multitude of claims for negligence against practising veterinary surgeons. Some of these were valid, but many were raised in hope or momentary anger and required tactful and often tedious handling. Letters to the legal profession were almost inevitably misunderstood due in the main to a perfectly reasonable lack of knowledge of the horse and also of the limits of scientific possibilities on their part. Even more, the over-hopeful expectations of their clients would often cloud the situation.

Now that retirement has finally arrived, a few of the more interesting and, I trust, amusing experiences can be told.

CHAPTER 1

Sortie to Scotland (1960's)

Although the majority of my expeditions beyond the limits of the practice were to those centres of bloodstock in France or Ireland, I occasionally ventured into the neighbouring, but to me equally foreign, countries which make up the United Kingdom.

Such a visit was arranged when I was contacted by an owner who was anxious to buy a promising steeplechaser in Scotland. As I had never been north of Yorkshire since my college days, I packed my overnight case with some excitement at the thought of an excursion into the land where whisky distilleries stood thicker on the ground than the pebbles on an English beach. My client had thoughtfully arranged for me to catch the overnight sleeper to Edinburgh, where I would be met by the trainer, one Willie Irvine. On enquiring at the local station, I was assured that a dining car would be available if I was to book when I reached London.

Shrugging on my overcoat since it was mid-February, I set off for the train to Paddington. It was my first train journey for several years, and my inexperience was only too obvious as I clambered on the first train to stop for London. I had allowed myself two and a half hours to catch the Scottish express and book my seat for dinner which by any stretch of the imagination was ample time. Alas, I had not reckoned on my ability to board the wrong train for a kick off. I settled back into my seat to enjoy the brief trip to London. To my surprise I had only just glanced at my book, when the train came to a sluggish halt. Looking out of the window I saw that we had gone some four miles and were standing at a wayside station, which I had believed to be long since defunct, a victim to Beeching, the decimator of the rural stations of England. So in this fashion we crawled on to the big city, making in all some nine stops. These halts seemed to be more in the nature of courtesy calls than for the purpose of moving the great British public about their business, since at no station did I see anybody enter or leave the train. True, I did have the chance to reminisce as we stayed for more than five minutes at Goring and Streatley station. Many was the time when I had hurried some young lady along the platform on our return from a dance in Reading, hoping that there was some chance of a night of bliss at my college digs in Streatley. But it seems that little changes with the passage of time. As in those days when most of my schemes for my creature comforts generally came to nought, so it appeared that my present plans for leisurely arrival for my dinner were to be thwarted as the minutes sped by with a frenetic rhythm that the train was in no mood to emulate.

Eventually arriving in London, I made my way to King's Cross for the night train to Edinburgh. Finding the correct platform, I boarded, and asked the somewhat lugubrious guard if the dining car was available. His expression brightened noticeably as he assured me that there was a dining car, which was open for those who had previously booked a meal. It soon became apparent that such a booking had to have been arranged before the departure of the train, and since we were already moving out of the station my chances were slim, even to say negligible. The dining car attendant was obviously intent on upholding the rigid rules of British Rail, stating that while you could eat with the train in motion, it was not permissible to order a meal once the wheels began to turn.

Despondent and hungry, I returned to my sleeper and managed to persuade the guard to dole me out a small packet of biscuits and a miniature bottle of whisky. So began my supposed exciting visit to the land of heather. Before finally seeking refuge from hunger in sleep, I asked if there was a likelihood of breakfast being served on board. Would it be necessary, I wondered, for me to wake up at three o'clock in the morning while the train was stationary in Newcastle station to place my order? With initial relief I learned that there was no need to order ahead, however my guardian pointed out with what seemed to be needless relish that this would only be available if I was continuing to Inverness. The train was due into Edinburgh at six o'clock, but as a generous concession I could stay on board until six thirty.

Sleepless and disenchanted, I lurched through the night, vowing yet again that I would never leave home for any far-distant location however tempting it might appear at the time. To add to my discomfort, not for the first time and very definitely not for the last, I singularly failed to master the temperature controls of my compartment. Pushing the lever to warm, I received a blast of roasting air. Easing it back to normal gave an icy stream that would have proved unwelcome even to a traveller in the Kalahari Desert. I could well add to the famous list of those whom Gilbert would not have missed, the designers of air conditioners to say nothing of manufacturers of showers.

Roused from an uneasy slumber which had finally overcome me at a quarter to six in the morning, I gathered up my case and emerged from the train. The car attendant wished me well and thanked me on behalf of British Rail. What had been positive about my company to earn this farewell I could not fathom, but as I was to discover later, when disembarking from a late arriving aircraft, it appeared to be the pious hope of some public relations man that if the staff were to pretend that the passenger's presence had given them intense pleasure, it would blot out the memory of any disasters which might have befallen him during his travel.

Awaiting me at the ticket barrier was an elderly man, dressed in a smart grey suit as though ready for a day at the office. Doffing his black trilby hat and with a bright smile he approached me.

"Good morning, Mr Frank. Welcome to Scotland."

I tried to smile back as convincingly as possible, and offering my hand in greeting said, "You must be Mr Irvine, I hope that you have not been waiting long."

The banality of this remark struck me even as I uttered it - how could anyone have been waiting for a long time to meet a train at such an ungodly hour?

Without a pause he seized my case and steered me to an old black Austin twelve of at least the 1935 vintage. I remembered many years ago learning to drive in such a vehicle, my instructor making me drive all the way down Dover Hill past the castle, towing a trailer to collect pig swill from the army camp during the war.

"Come on then," Mr Irvine laughed, "let us give you a taste of good Scottish sea air."

Sea air be damned, I would have settled for the taste of almost anything, but sea air did not promise much for my beleaguered stomach.

"We will drive straight to the stable so that you can see the horse. My son, Hamish, has him ready for you, so you can see him out on the sands where he can do a good gallop."

I nodded weakly and said that that sounded fine to me.

We drove for about an hour parallel to the railway line up which I had just come. We finally turned off the main road and drove down a long straight lane to a cluster of houses lying alongside the shore of an icy looking sea. It was a typical British seaside village. Bleak, but strong buildings built to withstand the bitter North Sea gales. Each house had a sign in the front window advertising rooms to let with board and bath extra. Apart from a training ground for Arctic explorers, I could not see much to tempt even the hardiest of long suffering holiday makers. Passing the local hostelry which was indistinguishable from the other boarding houses save for a swinging sign outside the door proclaiming it to be The Bonny Prince Charles Hotel, we turned into a yard and Mr Irvine stopped the engine.

"Wrap your coat around you," he grinned, "you southerners find our weather a mite fierce."

I climbed out of the car and was nearly blown off my feet by a howling wind straight off the sea. Willie Irvine propelled me forward towards a stable door behind the house. There he introduced me to Hamish, a small wiry fellow who had dispensed with every spare ounce of flesh, whether to ride the horse or to survive the cutting winds I could not say. Leaving me to follow his son, Willie disappeared into the house still looking sprightly and dapper enough to be a bank manager off to meet a long defaulting customer whose ship of fortune had at long last made port.

Hamish smiled engagingly and ushered me through a passage past three or four cage boxes with their inmates busy munching hay. He nodded towards them and said with a grin,

"They have earned their breakfast this morning, the sand was main heavy today after last night's high tide."

I could not believe that they had already finished their exercise for the day as it was still only just after eight o'clock.

"Oh yes," he assured me, "we always get them out at half past six as that allows me time to see to the shop before I go racing."

The shop, it transpired, was a highly skilled electronics business, which he had started in a shed up the road on his return from Stirling University some years before. He combined this successful enterprise with riding and caring for some fifteen racehorses. That was in no way to say that he played at training, since several Lambourn trainers knew to their cost that when the Irvines brought a horse south for one of the big handicaps it was one of which to be wary.

"You will like the big horse," he said as we passed through a small barn with boxes on either side of a central passage.

"He is a touch too good for us boys up here. He can live with our flat laddies on the sands - and jump, man, he could clear this house from a standstill."

Saying this he pushed back a box door and let me into a stable with a huge bay horse. He had a large star and a lot of white on his face, but otherwise not a white hair on his body. As I entered he pricked up his long curving ears and looked at me quizzically with his head slightly on one side as if to say, "What does this intrusion from the Sassenach mean at this hour of the morning?"

"He is a great character," laughed Hamish as he put on a headcollar, "he'll maybe not take kindly to strangers. You see, he has never been more than three miles from here except for the twice that he has raced."

I knew well about those occasions. He had cantered up in a novice hurdle at Wetherby even though he wandered from one side of the course to the other on the run-in from the last hurdle. In the second race he had jumped alongside the country's best novice hurdler from Yorkshire at the last hurdle and had stood off so far back that his luckless opponent fell through the jump trying to equal him.

I ran my hands down his legs and noticed a hard lump over the front of each of his fore fetlocks; otherwise he looked like an awkward big baby. We trotted him up the yard and then Hamish threw his saddle up onto the horse's mountainous back.

"I'll go on and father will bring you out in the car," he shouted against the wind as he headed out of the yard. As I turned, Willy Irvine came out of the house and beckoned me into the car. We turned out into the road and went along the shore lane to the sand dunes in the distance. Leaving the tarmac we lurched across the sand and grassy tussocks towards the beach. He pulled up within some ten feet of the sea itself and stopped the engine of the splendid old car.

"Right, we've got a wee walk to where Hamish will work past us."

I opened the door and had to lean my shoulder against it to force it open against the wind. By now I was in a state of semi-shock. Little sleep and nothing to eat since yesterday's snatched lunch - by God you wanted to be fit to survive in this place, no wonder the Scots live on porridge and malt whisky. Shrugging my too thin coat around my shoulders, I hurried over the dunes after Willy who had put on a light raincoat in deference to the howling blast.

We reached the edge of a long flat stretch of shining sand which seemed to go for a least a mile without any deviation. In the distance I saw Hamish on the horse thundering towards us. Even in my sorry state I felt an involuntary thrill at the way this gelding was eating up the ground. What a mover, he positively flowed over the sand. He came level with us and raced past throwing up a cloud of spray as he tore through the ebbing sea. Once past, Hamish stood up in the stirrups and shouted at Big Jamie to stop. Even as his words were flung back at us by the wind, the big horse slowed and wheeled round like a cat. He trotted back to where we stood, hardly out of breath although he must have galloped a good mile. I examined him, trying to shut out the scream of the elements from my stethoscope, and said we would meet him back in the stable.

Gratefully I returned to the warmth of the car. Willy gave a grin.

"He is some horse you know. But come on, I dare say you could eat a bit of toast with your coffee."

I nodded my agreement to both remarks and shut my eyes as the wheels spun in the sand and we reached for the road. If we had become stuck, I would have been as much use at pushing the car as an electric fire in Hell. Willy was quite unconcerned and as I discovered, he had trained horses on this piece of beach for the last thirty years, so he knew each tuft of grass like the back of his hand.

Once back at the stables Willy patted me on the back.

"You look to me as though a bite to eat might make you feel better disposed to our wild climate."

So saying, he led me into the kitchen, from where the aroma of bacon, eggs and sausage heralded hopes of renewed life. Half an hour later, replenished by an enormous meal and two cups of glorious hot coffee, I went out to renew my acquaintance with Big Jamie. With the exception of the lumps on his forelegs which I had noted previously, he was in perfect health. I returned to the house with Hamish and reported my conclusions.

"Never mind about those swellings," Willy said, "all my horses get something like that from working on the sand, but it never bothers them."

I had read of a similar injury affecting racehorses in America. They call them osselets, and they arise through continual galloping on firm dirt tracks. Comforted by the thought that it was not an unknown occurrence to the Irvines, I agreed they should have the joints x-rayed and if I was happy with the pictures I would advise my client to buy him. Secretly I was determined that he should not have the chance to miss buying one of the best young horses that I had seen for a long time.

Having completed my assignment Willy suggested that I should catch the train south from the local station. So at ten o'clock I once again entrusted myself to British Rail.

"It's a stopping train I am afraid," shouted the trainer as I opened the carriage door.

"Don't worry about that," I answered. "I am quite used to those."

This time the stops were at intervals of fifty miles rather than five as before, and the dining car was available to all travellers. I eventually picked up my car at ten o'clock that night and gratefully drove home.

The next morning I drove into the yard in Lambourn to be met by the usual snide remarks, which greeted anyone who had strayed beyond the practice boundaries. Despite vigorous denials it was generally considered that a day away was a holiday and therefore something to be paid for on return to the daily routine.

Sortie to Scotland

The first to accost me was Johnny Healey, our yard man and general factotum. Demanding at least a look at the mythical bottle of Scotch, which he was sure I had been given, he approached the car with a broad grin. Johnny was an Irishman, an excellent horseman who had served his time in racing stables before coming to us from a fill-in job digging the new sewer ditches in the village. There seemed to be nobody in racing whom he did not know, and he would engage top trainers and racing lads equally in conversation as they walked into the surgery.

In those days all the big veterinary practices had such a man, who in may ways ran the affairs of the vets. He would answer the telephone calls from the clients and arrange who was to visit them and at what time of day. Johnny was invaluable to us for his skill in holding and quietening difficult horses during treatment. His constant flow of Irish expressions kept the animals engaged and us entertained. With a specially awkward colt he would assure us that the animal was so weak that it would not even pull the socks off a dead man. During my thirty years or so in the practice we were served by only two yard men, Johnny having taken up the reins when old Jim Enoch retired. Jim himself had joined my predecessors in the early nineteen twenties. As a raw veterinary student he had taught me a lot about horses and, more importantly, racing folk.

Escaping from Healey, I went into the office only to be accosted by John, our new assistant. A lad from Cumbria, he was convinced that all southerners had life easy and were not used to the hard grind of his native Cockermouth. After you had survived a particularly strenuous day spent rasping teeth in a jumping yard, he would tell you how he had passed his youth following the fell hounds around his home and why were you feeling exhausted? Regretfully this all bounced back on him, as we set out to keep him as busy as possible, which I believe persuaded him to keep from irritating remarks about the soft living in Berkshire.

As I walked to the telephone he muttered that he too would like a day travelling to Scotland. Remembering the vicissitudes of the past twenty four hours, I felt he was more than welcome. Leaving him to his grievances I phoned the prospective owner of Big Jamie to let him know of my findings. I explained that while I had loved the horse I would not be happy until I had seen the x-rays of his front legs. I had known the client for some two years, and well realised that he was a most difficult man. He had changed his trainers as often as most people change their shirts. He had moved his five horses down to a trainer in Chepstow where he had enjoyed considerable success. I had entered his life when asked to see a Champion Hurdle winner who had suffered a fracture of the long bone above the hock. In the sixties, before the era of equine surgery, conservative treatment was the routine. In the main this entailed rest and a lot of patience. Fortunately in this case the cure was successful, with the horse winning his third Champion Hurdle at Cheltenham the following year. As a result I was still the favourite boy, but I certainly did not wish to risk any mistakes.

Three days after my return, the x-rays arrived from Scotland. As Willy Irvine had assured me, the injuries were indeed old and unlikely to cause any problems in the future. Relaying the good news to my man, he asked me to arrange to have the horse sent down to Wales without delay. Big Jamie duly arrived at his new quarters, where the trainer was thankfully delighted with him. He went on to prove every bit as successful as I had hoped, winning eleven races for his owner in the next four seasons. Each time he won I would receive a call from Hamish to say how pleased he was and what a bargain he had proved for the present trainer.

An unfortunate sequel to all this was to happen three years later. I was out on my rounds when Johnny Healey rang to ask what he was to do with four horses which had just been delivered to the yard for my care. Having been given no warning of any horses coming to the surgery, I enquired which they were, what they had arrived for and who owned them. Johnny said they had come from Wales and looked so fit that he did not feel that my veterinary skill was necessary, but could I please return quickly as the police were standing in the yard and getting under his feet. With that I turned the car round and headed over the Downs as speedily as I could.

When I got out of the car I looked at the horses and immediately recognised Big Jamie as one of the quartet. It transpired that the owner had fallen out with the trainer and had summarily removed the horses without a word to anybody in the stables. Why they had been sent to me was a mystery, but on the trainer's return from the gallops he had alerted the police that they had been stolen. Pleading total ignorance to the local constabulary, I tried to placate both the trainer and the owner with, I am afraid, no great success. The final outcome was that the four horses departed to Epsom and with them went a police escort to see fair play.

Their departure to the new surroundings terminated my connection with that particular owner - a split that did not unduly worry me, since my feelings were very much on the side of the trainer, who had done a splendid job with the horses. My only sorrow was the severing of my dealings with the horse who had taken me to the northern part of the British Isles, where I had been given some inkling of the tough surroundings in which racing operated in that, to us, distant area.

CHAPTER 2

Forays to France (1960's)

As I have said, life in a busy practice is pretty hectic and there is always more work on hand than can be comfortably coped with. For this reason the announcement that you were going out of the area for a day was likely to be greeted with a jaundiced eye by your colleagues. The general feeling was that a jaunt off anywhere beyond a fifteen mile radius of Lambourn was going to prove more like a bank holiday outing than work. This particularly applied if you were seen rooting about the office for passports and foreign currency.

The truth of the matter was somewhere in between. Usually the venture would involve meeting new faces and seeing interesting horses, but the travel always seemed to come back to the same incessant race against the clock. A day in Chantilly conjured up optimistic thoughts of svelte French mademoiselles, escargots and Mouton Rothschild. The illusions however were quickly shattered as you crawled out of bed at five o'clock in the morning and drove up the M4 to Heathrow in time to catch the seven o'clock flight to Paris. The exciting plastic airline breakfast was barely sufficient to keep you alive until landing and certainly did little to raise the flagging spirits. Once out of the airport you fell into the grasp of a voluble Frenchman who carried you at breakneck speed through the rush hour traffic to the stable.

The general scheme of French trainers seemed to be that of trying to completely demoralise you before you even arrived at the stable. The driver was selected not only for his apparent disregard of all traffic regulations and his total lack of any English, but also for his capacity to chain smoke Gaulois whilst simultaneously gnawing at a choice slice of garlic salami. Once at the stable you stumbled out of the car in a bemused state to be met by an obviously over-pressed trainer, who cast a cursory look at you and apologised for having to rush off to see a new owner. Pointing at a small youth who was to be your guide, jockey and

general comforter, he would jump into his car with a parting question,
"Parlez-vous Français, j'espère?"

Without waiting for your protestations that his hopes were in vain, he would disappear off in a cloud of dust.

The initial examination of what you hope was the correct horse presented few problems, since muttered phrases such as *"Faites-vous lui marcher"* or *"Faites lui trotter"* usually had the desired effect even though your accent was even more dubious than your grammar. However, the troubles arising from an attempt at fixing a rendez-vous on the gallops to see the horse in action made you wonder why you had not opted for a quiet day rasping teeth in a Lambourn stable. On one occasion I waved down a rider on a chestnut horse as he cantered past me on a sand gallop, and to his stupefaction ordered him off his horse and proceeded to apply my stethoscope to the horse's chest. It took several noisy minutes before I realised that I had captured a horse from a totally different stable. I was only saved from some dire fate when the horse's trainer arrived and sorted out my predicament, sending me on my way to another track through the trees where I found my target walking around, having completed his exercise undisturbed by me.

Once having finished the examination and come to a conclusion as to whether the horse was suitable for the English client, the ability of the stable staff to speak and understand English would miraculously return. Any response to queries as to whether the animal was all right or not, would be greeted with a further torrent of French extolling its undoubted virtues. Should the decision be a thumbs down, you were likely to find yourself back in the car, being conveyed even faster to the airport despite protestations that the plane did not take off for a least four hours. However if the decision was in the affirmative, all was hospitality... coffee, cognac and cigars would be produced. The trainer would make a surprise early return from his new owner, and a gargantuan lunch would be offered. This time any protests that the plane was due to take off in one hour would be brushed aside, as more cognac was called for. In this case the journey back to the airport would be even more frantic, and you would stumble up the aircraft steps under the disapproving stares of the plane staff, who had been kept waiting by your late arrival.

Back in England the journey home seemed interminable as you fought off sleep and the after-effects of good living. As you walked into the house, the phone would ring with one of the practice members, who could not wait to tell you with the air of a martyr, how he had struggled through the day tending all of your misdiagnosed cases. The morning after such a venture would not be improved by the unsubtle winks and nudges from the rest of the practice as they pleaded exhaustion and so could not dash off themselves to attend to a colic case in an unbroken colt.

During my time in Lambourn, visits such as these to France were not uncommon, but they usually involved horses which were kept in the better known stables of Chantilly. So it was interesting to receive a phone call from a trainer friend of mine asking me to accompany him to see some horses in Maisons-Laffitte. Sydney was of French parentage with a French wife, who was charming and, needless to say, an excellent cook. He had begun life in Paris with his father, who trained horses there. Syd had graduated to become a professional jockey on the Paris circuit before coming to England to try his luck at training. His methods were nothing if not unorthodox. His idea of working his horses was to canter them up a steep hill, which was not in itself unusual, but his choice of canter was up the centre of the old A34 trunk road from Birmingham to Southampton. At that time in the early sixties there was no by-pass around the village where he trained, so that he would lead up a string of ten horses against a stream of heavy traffic bound for the continent on one of the busiest roads in England. Questioned as to why he preferred this hazardous exercise ground, he replied that the level tarmac was safer for his horses legs than the rough ground of his unkempt gallop. In addition to his training methods he had incurred the suspicion of the racing authorities over some doubtful form of his winners.

On this occasion he had an order to buy two horses, which would make dual purpose animals. That is to say they should be able to run both on the flat and also over hurdles with some hope of winning a few contests. Having agreed to accompany Syd on this outing we duly met at the customary ungodly hour at Heathrow. We were to meet some of his old racing acquaintances in the less fashionable training area of Maisons-Laffitte.

It was no surprise therefore to find that our first call was to a seedy-looking character, dressed in a jacket and trousers which looked as if they had been borrowed from the local rubbish tip. Sucking on a Gaulois, he invited us in for a welcome cup of strong black coffee. I drank this while the two trainers talked in voluble French presumably about the evil doings of the racing establishment, whom they considered were a hindrance to their quite reasonable ploys of defeating the bookmakers. Having aired their respective grievances, Monsieur Defart suggested we go and see the two horses, which he considered to be a perfect answer to my friend's search.

The first horse was a big ungainly five year old gelding with a head that would have done justice to a Shire horse. At first glance in the stable I could see that the poor horse was the owner of not one but two bowed tendons on his forelegs. I nudged Syd (by the way, not a very French name for my French friend) and glanced towards the legs. He signalled by a lift of his eyebrows that he too had seen the afflictions. Despite our obvious lack of enthusiasm, Monsieur Defart insisted on bringing his pride and joy out of the stable for our further inspection. This was not a wise ploy as it was plain to see that the horse was lame as soon as he was encouraged to trot. Syd gave the thumbs down sign and the horse was reluctantly returned to his stable.

Undaunted the trainer lead us to another box, and with a Gallic flourish ushered us in to see a grey filly, who would not have looked out of place at any Pony Club. Seeing our disappointment, the proud trainer launched off to explain that what she lacked in size she more the compensated by having the heart of a lion. Since she was hardly strong enough to carry a very light teenager, she must indeed have possessed a heart large enough to warrant an entry in the Guinness Book of Records.

Syd apologised for wasting his friend's time, and we once more got into the car. This performance was repeated four more times before lunch. I had never before seen this side of French racing, although I knew plenty of English counterparts. Syd explained after the last fruitless visit that most of his old acquaintances were of the struggling variety, and only too anxious to unload at least one of their disasters onto their so-called friend. I am not sure why I had not realised that there would be so many damaged, bad horses, but I had only seen the prosperous side of racing on my previous visits. The French vets were plainly kept busy in this area, but whether they managed to draw any money from their clients was a moot point.

After restoring ourselves with an excellent lunch I asked whether our journey was not going to be in vain. Assured that we still had some other nuggets to unearth, we set off for the next assignment. As we drove into the yard my spirits lifted a little. At least the buildings looked an improvement. In fact the trainer's house seemed more like the abode of a wealthy owner than a horse trainer. A knock on the door brought out a dapper little man, dressed in cavalry twill trousers and a smart brown tweed jacket. Indeed the expected clothing for a successful trainer. Syd introduced himself, and the trainer welcomed us into the house. Unlike those of our morning calls, the furnishings would have done more than justice to the pages of Country Life. The hall was embellished with several excellent oil paintings of equestrian scenes, and the hall table and dresser might well have come from Versailles. Possibly they had, since the drawing room into which Monsieur de Forget lead us had a splendid fireplace surmounted by an elegant gilt plaster Louis XV mirror.

Coffee was offered and served in a silver coffee pot of Italian design. Such was the splendour of the house that I began to wonder if any horse there could possibly be within my friend's limited budget. Finishing the coffee we were taken out to the immaculately swept yard. Monsieur de Forget had earmarked two possible horses for sale. The first was a four year old bay colt, standing sixteen and a half hands high at the withers, with a bold eye and those attractive ears with a slight backward curve, which seems to signify the French Thoroughbred. The colt was lead out of his box and moved up the yard with a majestic stride. The trainer told us that the colt had won two races at Longchamp over the equivalent distance of one and a quarter miles. The second horse was a smaller three year old gelding, which had won three races on the flat and one over hurdles at Auteuil. Not so impressive as the first, but nevertheless a tough workmanlike horse with an easy loping stride.

The horses were saddled up after I had made a brief examination of each in the stable. Jumping into the trainer's car, and old black Citroen of a type now out of fashion in England but still serviceable for driving on the gallops. During the journey to the exercise grounds Monsieur de Forget reminded Syd of how my friend had decanted him at the last hurdle when he was about to overtake Syd's horse.

Apparently he had at that time been the leading amateur jockey in France and as such was considered fair game by a professional jockey such as Sydney. I was about to say that my friend's habits had not much altered since he moved to England, when my arm was nudged and I was given a warning glance. Questioning my companion later, it transpired that it had taken a great deal of persuasion for the authorities not to suspend his licence and take the race off him. The difficulty had come about due to the stipendiary steward being Monsieur de Forget's brother. It was felt that that prosecution of Syd might smack just a little of nepotism.

We arrived through the woods at a length of grass gallops, which were clearly tended with much loving care and attention. Would that many of our home racecourses had received similar good husbandry. The jockeys cantered down to the start of a straight five furlong track, wheeled around, and followed each other up towards us at a respectful distance apart. At home the lads would have vied with each other to take the lead and more than likely would have passed me together, making it impossible to listen to their individual breathing. The colt led the way, but his rider was having a difficult job to restrain his mount from bounding away from his companion. Both horses satisfied me that their breathing was perfectly normal and their hearts were beating regularly and quickly showed signs of returning to the usual resting speed. This indicated that the two were fit and ready for a race.

Making our way back to the stables we were taken on a tour of the training area. This was remarkable to me for the variety of differing tracks, mostly through the thick woods. Some were grass, but a number were sand tracks like those I had seen in Chantilly. As yet we had not arrived at the practice of working horses at home on all weather tracks. A team of groundsmen were busy harrowing and rolling the gallops after the morning's activity.

Back in the yard, I made a detailed examination of each horse. I felt able to pronounce that the two seemed in good order with considerably less difficulty than is often customary. Passing the glad tidings to Syd we followed Monsieur de Forget back into this delightful house. It was now nearly half past four and our plane was due to leave Paris at six o'clock, so I hoped that the negotiations would not be too lengthy. Alas, the asking price was half as much again as Syd had hoped to pay. This brought about a heated period of horse trading, lubricated with some excellent Bisquet de Bouche, which I personally much enjoyed while leaving the two contestants to continue their bargaining in voluble French. Three quarters of an hour later, to my evident relief they shook hands on a deal which apparently suited them both.

With now only forty five minutes left to catch our plane, Syd set off at a pace similar to that of a Formula One driver. We sped around the Périphérique, usually on the correct side of the road, although my eyes were tightly shut for most of the trip. Syd was delighted with his day in Paris, and kept assuring me that he had succeeded in getting the price down to several hundred francs below what he thought he would have to pay.

At Le Bourget we just made our plane, even though they had to re-open the cabin door to let us fall in. Dropping into my seat, to my horror my companion ordered two large brandies to celebrate our purchases. On my other side in the plane was a dear old lady who engaged me in conversation. She explained that she was an American going to London to see her married daughter. I asked if she was being met at the airport and she said she would have to find a taxi. I offered to give her a lift to town, where I was spending the night with my parents. Putting her in the passenger seat, I drove through the tunnel under the runway. I heard what I took to be a telephone ringing but I emerged from the tunnel to be overtaken by a police car with its siren screaming. Pulling into the side, I rolled down the window to be greeted by an irate policeman. Had I not heard their siren and why had I not stopped? I did not dare to say that I thought I had heard a telephone ringing. This would have really brought the wrath of the law down on me, especially as I was breathing out of a strong aroma of brandy (thank heavens this occurred long before the days of breathalysers). Apologising profusely, I explained that I had to deliver my companion to her daughter with all haste. He took my address and cautioned me on the dangers of fast driving and let me drive on. Fast driving indeed, he should have been with me in Paris to see some really speedy motoring.

Getting to town I arrived at the address of the lady's destination. As I stepped out of the car, she passed me a paperback book, which she explained was her latest work. Not until I got home did I look at this. To my amazement the cover was that of a semi-naked girl with a knife stuck through her ribs. The title being "Death in a Dingy Apartment". When I turned the cover over I found that this was the fourteenth book written by my dear old lady. It turned out to be every bit as lurid a read as the cover had promised. You can never tell anybody's occupation by their looks!

The result of our day in France was highly successful. The gelding won three races at prices which indicated that Syd had more than paid for his visit. The colt proved even more of a bargain than had been hoped. He won two good races on the flat and finished third in the Champion Hurdle at Cheltenham the next year. After three seasons racing he retired to stud to become a successful National Hunt stallion. Altogether a satisfactory and most entertaining visit to La Belle France.

It was some years later in 1977, when a new disease affecting breeding stock afflicted a number of studs in England, that I returned once again to France. The causal organism of the infection took some time to identify as it was a hitherto unrecognised bacterium. The infection was causing infertility in the mares and was spread from one mare to another by the stallions. Along with two Welsh colleagues I was asked to produce a Code of Practice for the management of this disease. One year after the outbreak at home, the disease was recognised on some studs in France.

The French breeders requested that the British Thoroughbred Breeders' Association should send two of their representatives to explain the rationale of the Code to their vets and stud managers. Thus it was that Dai, one of the Welsh colleagues, and I met at Cambridge airport one morning to fly in a private plane owned by a trainer friend of mine. While it was not uncommon for some of the leading jockeys to own their own aircraft, trainers usually had to make do with road transport. However my friend had been lucky enough to win the Derby the previous year which explained his obvious affluence.

Neither Dai nor I were very experienced in small aircraft flights, so it was with some apprehension that we took our seats. My only previous encounter with this means of travel had been some years previously when I flew with a trainer to France in a single-engined plane. I spent the whole of that journey with my eyes glued to the propeller, willing it to keep spinning. The flight to Deauville was fortunately uneventful with our two experienced pilots, and we arrived safely to be met by a well known French breeder, who whisked us off to an excellent lunch accompanied by some very drinkable white wine. This was my first mistake of the day since following the meal, my chief thoughts centred on sleep rather than an important meeting.

We arrived at the French National Stud, an imposing small chateau built in the shape of an "E" without the centre line. The two sides stretching from the main building housed the many stallions which were kept by the State for the benefit of the farmer breeders and were sent out to different areas of the country. Breeds varied from large

Percherons to Thoroughbreds with a number of Selle Français, a breed which I had not come across before. Basically used for breeding, riding and performance horses, they were later to be recognised at home as sires of very useful steeplechasers.

Our guide ushered us into a large meeting room in the chateau, where we were confronted by some twenty men, mainly breeders but also a considerable leavening of veterinary surgeons. The meeting began with the chairman welcoming the two of us and asking whether we could follow if the proceedings were conducted in French. Foolishly I made my second mistake of the day by agreeing that I believed we could understand the drift of what would be discussed. They then proceeded to set out their problem and what they felt should be done to stop the spread of the disease. I nudged Dai to see if he was understanding the conversation. He lent over and whispered that he could not understand any French at all. This did little to ease my growing fear that our visit was going to be a fiasco. At this point one of the senior vets, whom I had known for many years, realised our predicament and offered to translate the salient points of the discussion. After half an hour the chairman suggested that the meeting be adjourned so that the veterinary element could move to another room to discuss the scientific necessities of any control measures. With six colleagues, Dai and I made for a small circular room at the foot of one of the turrets of the building.

"I think that our fate is now somewhat akin to those being thrown into the Tower of London in Tudor days. I trust we shall not end up on the scaffold," I warned Dai as the door closed behind us.

It was one thing trying to follow a general discourse on breeding problems, but quite another when our opposite numbers launched off into voluble arguments full of technical terminology. In vain did we try to explain in English what control measures had been imposed successfully at home. The gist of the argument seemed to be that if our control was so good, why had some UK mares taken the disease to France? Thankfully before the entente cordiale became irredeemably destroyed my French friend, who had taken over the role of interpreter, announced that he had recognised this disease several years previously on local studs in Normandy. I was not sure that I agreed with him but I was relieved to latch onto this argument to preserve international relations. In this we were successful, since the talk then centred on which French stud had been responsible for keeping its problem out of the public domain.

Before the meeting could break up with total discord, I suggested in my very halting French that we should return to the question of what action should be taken. I felt that if we proceeded as we were going little would be achieved or, worse still, Dai and I might agree unwittingly to something which our linguistic deficiencies had led us to misunderstand.

"Would it not be better," I asked, "if we were to write our suggestions in French when we returned home and send these for your approval?"

I was sure that we could find some kind soul in Newmarket who could translate our English Code into reasonable French.

To my relief, Dai agreed to organise this, and further the idea seemed to meet with approval from the remainder of the vets. With smiles all round we returned to the main meeting. The chairman accepted our suggestions and called for coffee and cognac for all to signal the end of what for me had been an exhausting day. I never realised the strain imposed in trying for several hours to patch together the gist of a meeting carried out in a foreign tongue. After the refreshments our guide took us back to his car to return to his own stud farm. On the way he profusely apologised that he had to return to Paris, but he assured us that bedrooms were at our disposal and dinner had been arranged. Thus we found ourselves alone in the fine eighteenth century chateau, with access to an excellent dinner. This was a life to which we could very easily become accustomed.

Next morning we came down to a strong cup of coffee, and were summoned to the door by one of the stud staff who had been asked to show us round the magnificent stud. There were four stallions out in their separate paddocks. The mares and young stock were happily grazing in the further paddocks. The whole scene was one of tranquillity. Everywhere looked immaculate despite the fall of autumn leaves. The buildings were of that lovely half-timbered design so indicative of Normandy. The stud had been commandeered during the war for the headquarters of the German army in that area. They certainly knew which place to choose. Unfortunately they left the chateau and buildings in total disarray and it had taken the present owner ten or more years to restore it to its eighteenth century magnificence.

When we walked back to the front door a car awaited us to go back to our plane. Feeling like royalty Dai and I clambered on board. This time the flight was not so serene as that of the previous day. Turbulence was the order of the day and we bucketed home across the Channel, both of us regretting the dinner of the evening before. Even so we duly arrived back in Cambridge and drove on to Newmarket. We were greeted by the usual remarks of "Easy money for you lucky couple". Little did they know that we felt that we had more than earned every penny by saving the friction between our neighbours across the water and in reaching a degree of satisfactory harmony.

At that time I was unaware that nearly twenty years on I was to perform that same retrieval of the entente cordiale. Yet again another dispute over the interpretation of the dreaded Code of Practice was to cause annoyance to our Gallic friends. It first happened when I was chairing a breeders' meeting in Deauville. All went well until one of the French vets stood up and attacked the British and Irish for misleading the local breeders over one of the requirements in the Code. Unlike previous times this concerned a different venereal disease known as Equine Virus Arteritis which had caused havoc in Kentucky in the early eighties and had suddenly emerged in England in 1995. Because of this, English breeders were not unnaturally keen to ensure that visiting mares were free of the disease. The test entailed the taking of a blood sample after arrival at the stallion's stud.

The French decided that we were being bloody-minded and thus costing their breeders extra money in keep for the mares. Putting his argument vehemently he began to shout at me. Quietly trying to assuage him, I pointed out that we had historically won the battle of Waterloo, and I was not averse to having a replay. Fortunately feelings calmed down over a good lunch and several glasses of Calvados, the local strong beverage.

I agreed to return home and consider the position and then to come back and talk to their breeders. On reflection I felt that regrettably there had been a degree of xenophobia on the part of the British studs and we were able to reach a happy compromise. My one attempt at diplomacy seemed to have paid off well and I was inordinately pleased with myself. No doubt my successor will once again have to pick up the pieces of the next problem. The European Union undoubtedly affects all spheres of life.

CHAPTER 3

Wandering in Wales (1960's)

I first visited the Principality many years ago, when I set off to examine a point-to-point horse in Pembrokeshire, 'that little England beyond Wales' which no self-respecting Welshman will admit to having seen. It was a case of love at first sight for me - the sweeping hills, majestically guarding the green fertile valleys. Only a stone's throw from the scarred ridges of the Rhondda, but literally in another world. The tough, quick farmers with their unnerving ability to switch from Welsh to English in mid-sentence without a pause. Used to a hard life working the hills with their sheep and ponies, they have the gift to play as hard as they work. Many is the time since my first visit that I have crept back down the motorway to England, exhausted and bewildered by their seemingly total lack of the need for sleep.

One of the attractions of Wales for me is the complete unpredictability of its inhabitants. On my journey up to see my point-to-pointer I called in to see an elderly man near Sennybridge who had two chasers in training with a friend of mine.

"Do look him up, and take him this Stilton cheese," I was instructed. "He is a man of few words but he will be sure to give you a good welcome."

So armed with the cheese and Mr Morgan's unpronounceable address I enquired at the first pub in the town for his farm.

"Going to see old Dai Morgan are you?" said the landlord. "Better mind his dogs, they've had more people than I have had fish out of the Usk," he laughed.

Thanking him for his warning I wound my way up a high banked lane that clung to the side of the valley. After three miles I saw a dilapidated old square-built house lying up a weed strewn drive. Pulling up outside the steps to the front door, I hooted my horn to alert the dogs and awaited the onslaught. Nothing happened so I cautiously opened the car door and pressed the door bell. After a couple of minutes the door was eased open by an elderly lady, who seemed to be dressed in clothing straight out of a Dickens novel. I gave my name and asked if Mr Morgan was at home.

"I'll go and see," she answered and closed the door again.

Within a minute she was back and the door swung open to release a pair of enormous bull mastiffs, who thankfully charged straight past me having missed my rapid jump onto the narrow balustrade by the door.

"Lord love you," said Mrs Gamp with a smile, "they will not harm you, it's the terrier who will have you when he sees you, but he is with his master."

I was ushered into the hall, past portraits of previous generations of Morgans and two priceless Welsh dressers, and on to the drawing room. Dai Morgan rose to greet me, extending a welcoming hand and, I was glad to notice, a warning shoe towards the terrier who retired growling behind a sofa. My host was a man in his late seventies, I guessed, garbed in an old worn pair of grey flannels and an even more decrepit pair of carpet slippers. Above the trousers he wore an ageing collarless shirt with one sleeve secured to the rest of the shirt by a large safety pin.

Hoping that this unlikely looking gentleman was in fact my friend's owner of the two best steeplechasers in his yard, I proffered the Stilton and introduced myself. Mr Morgan's face suddenly became alive with a mischievous grin.

"So you are Tom's vet, are you, I hope that those two horses of mine are fit and well. I am relying on big things from The King."

I assured him that when I had last seen King Jester two days ago he was a picture of health.

"Good," he replied, "I have just put a thousand pounds on him to win that chase at Newbury. I got sixteen to one, I did."

Well, I knew that Tom had said he liked to let the old boy have a gamble or two, but from the look of his clothing I would have thought that a fiver would be his maximum investment.

Telling me to wait, he shuffled off to find me a drink. As I was left on my own, the terrier thankfully having followed his master, I idly glanced at the book which he had been reading as I entered the room. To my surprise it was an old copy of Racine's Phaedre. Even more to my amazement it was in the original French. I wandered over to the bookshelves and saw that there were rows of old copies of the French classics, all printed and published in France. When he returned I could not help asking him how he had come to be a French scholar. Self-taught, he replied with a grin. It transpired that he had bought a job lot of books many years ago in the Abergavenny auction rooms and finding that they were all written in French he had decided to learn the language rather than waste the money he had spent on them. He brushed aside my curiosity as to his linguistic accomplishments and launched into an encyclopedic analysis of the current jumping form in Britain and Ireland.

Three whiskys later and with darkness descending I got up to take my leave of this surprising paradox of a man. As I went to get into the car he pushed a paper package into my hand.

"Take that my boy, and look after the King well. It's fair exchange for Tom's cheese."

I took the parcel and put it over on the back seat where a large salmon slid out of it onto my suitcase. As an introduction into the anomalies of Wales I could not have found a better example. Kind, shrewd, miserly, generous - all of them were wrapped up in the spare frame of this scholarly old gentleman.

I had planned to stay at the main hotel in Llandovery for the night, but first I had to call in at a little old pub at the far end of the town. A great friend of mine was a schoolmaster who loved his racing. Some thirty years before he had been on the staff of Llandovery College, and he had made a few wise but many more foolish investments with a character called Willy Isaacs. Willy, I understood, had combined the roles of bookie's runner, poacher and general rogue with his duties as college caretaker. I was sure that thirty years must have seen a change in Willy's drinking habits even if not his actual demise, but my friend insisted that I should at least enquire. I pushed open the door of the saloon bar and ordered a beer from the landlady. I asked her if she had ever heard of a man called Willy Isaac.

"Yes, bless you, he is in the public with Jones the bailiff. Why don't you go through?"

I took my glass and went into the other bar. There were two men sitting by the fireplace. One was tall and gaunt, the other short and stout with a red face and a slight cast in his left eye. I introduced myself and explained that I had been told not to dare to pass Llandovery without looking up Mr Isaac. At this the stout man raised himself from his stool and shook my hand. I then explained further that my friend Joe Knight had asked me to give him his regards. I was about to go on to jog his memory about Joe when he threw back his head and chuckled.

"There now, I haven't seen old Joe for a few weeks it seems. How is the old devil, still teaching his boys how to count by giving them his betting slips for them to add up?"

Saying that 'the few weeks' were more like thirty years, but that Joe's teaching habits had not materially altered, Willy then continued pumping my hand up and down muttering,

"Dhu, dhu there's a thing now. Fancy old Joe still minding me. You ask him if he still gets his feet wet on his evening walks?"

At this remark the tall companion coughed, and Willy looked across at him with a sly grin,

"All right, Emrys, it was only looking after your river that we used to be. If a sewin happened to jump up on the bank by our feet, who was to blame us? Anyway my old rheumatics stop me going near the damp these days."

Emrys Jones, the local water bailiff, gave a disbelieving grunt but volunteered that it was his round and he would fill our glasses. While he was away at the bar Willy winked at me and asked if I could call in again tomorrow lunchtime.

"You call in, bach, and ask Maggie at the bar for a parcel for old Joe. I am sure that I can manage to find something that will remind him of past days in Llandovery."

I spent another hour in the company of the two men and heard more tales of gambles accomplished by local sportsmen, and other extra-mural activities which led me to believe that Willy Isaac has not forsaken his old habits. I duly called in the next day and received two parcels from Maggie. Parcels remarkably similar to the one that I had been given by Dai Morgan. Despite my offer, she said that not a penny would he take.

"It wasn't as though they had cost him much, now, had they," she added with a laugh.

I eventually arrived at my destination near Milford Haven. It was pelting with rain and a sea fog was blowing in across the estuary. I drove into a little stable yard at the rear of the house and was greeted by the owner, a tall imposing man with only one arm. He led me into a loose box where stood a fine looking grey horse. I knew that he had won two races at local hunt meetings - an encouraging start for a five year old horse. I looked him over and said that we had better get him out and listen to his wind before the fog closed in completely. The owner threw his saddle over the horse's back and expertly did up the girth and martingale, despite being single-handed. I mentioned this to him and he laughed, saying that practice made him perfect since he had lost his arm in a fishing accident at sea over forty years ago. I offered to ride the horse, rather than wait for his groom to arrive.

"Groom be damned," he answered, "can't afford one of those now with these high wages at the oil terminal. No, I'll ride him for you, you might get lost and end up in the sea."

So saying he pulled the gelding into the yard and vaulted into the saddle with the agility of a boy a generation younger. As he trotted out of the yard I followed him in the now torrential rain, running lest I lose the two of them in the mist.

The horse was keen and took a great hold of his bit as they turned into a small two acre field, bordered on two sides by sheer cliffs to the murky sea below. I immediately understood why he was not keen for me to be the jockey. Without another word the rider, clad in his tweed suit with a short waist length mackintosh against the elements, broke into a fast canter. With no difficulty he rode the horse around the corners of the field, moving his arm from side to side as though steering an old fashioned tram. Hearing nothing wrong with the horse's breathing, I suggested that we retreat to the shelter of the stable. As I walked behind I remembered that the horse had no shoes on his hind feet. As the owner dismounted I asked why he was not shod behind. He explained that it was easier for him to get a grip on the roads without the shoes and anyway blacksmiths were hard to come by in that area. This all seemed slightly unlikely, but I let it pass and began to examine the horse. All went well until I reached the hind legs. I picked up the left hind and felt down the tendons and joints, then went around to repeat the procedure on the other side. Although I tugged at the leg and offered encouraging remarks to the horse there was no way I could get the horse to lift the right hind leg. I managed to lift it about three inches off the ground, only for him to slam it down again, narrowly missing my fingers.

I turned to the owner, who apologised for forgetting to tell me that he had never trained the horse to lift his right leg, since with his one arm he could not manage to raise it properly. I sympathised and said something to the effect that he appeared to cope well without it. Never taught it indeed! There was no way that education would have improved matters, since the animal was patently unable to lift that leg due to a nervous disability rather than lack of training. So that was why he had no shoes on his hind feet. The blacksmith had obviously come up against the same problem. Once again I went to lift the leg, but this time I watched the muscles over his quarters. As soon as I touched his fetlock there were the tell-tale signs of the shivering of the muscles above. He was undoubtedly a bad 'shiverer', and as such totally unsuitable as a racehorse. The condition would not probably affect his jumping, but unless he could be shod all round he was only going to be a liability in a racing stable.

I thanked the man and complimented him on the condition of his horse and told him I would report to my client, who would no doubt be in touch on the telephone. Excusing myself, I set off home feeling that the whole outing had been a wild goose chase. Somehow it always felt much more worthwhile when a horse you went to examine was satisfactory, since your client had something to show for the visit. In fact it was probably much more valuable when you saved him from buying an unsuitable animal.

Some months after my visit to Milford Haven I received a telephone call from a very good acquaintance of mine, Evan Davies, who was a vet in that part of Wales where an Englishman feels that he needs a passport to enter. The inhabitants only regard the English as cannon fodder for the Arms Park and the national rugby team. My wife Wendy had, for some time, embarked on the foundation of a Welsh Pony stud. This venture had a reluctant interest from me initially, but when I discovered that it involved fairly frequent tours to studs in the depths of Wales, my enthusiasm quickened. The main result of these excursions was that Wendy and I gathered many extremely good friends in the hills of Powys and Dyfed. A rather more unexpected result was that the continuing presence of a racing vet from Berkshire became a topic of conversation in the hostelries which were threaded like jewels along the length of the A40, that thrombosed artery of a highway through the centre of South Wales, now thankfully superceded by the larger motorway.

Following one of those convivial evenings, the suggestion was mooted to Evan Davies, the local vet, that he should persuade me to come up and operate on two horses in the area. I heard of this request with a slightly sinking heart. I did not consider myself to be one of God's surgeons, indeed I had been gifted with five thumbs on each hand: a theory to which I may say my wife subscribes whole-heartedly following one of my many attempts to mend a cupboard or a light fitting. Further I was of the opinion that surgery was far better undertaken behind the closed doors of your own establishment, where at least the patient is close at hand during the all-important and often worrying recovery period.

However there was to be no way that I could refuse my friends, and neither operation was more than routine. Feeling braver than I should have done I fixed a day when Evan would ring up, and left him to make all the arrangements. The night before the appointed time I collected all the necessary instruments and phoned again to see if there was any hope of a last minute reprieve.

"No chance boy, everything is laid on and we are looking forward to seeing you in action."

"What do you mean by 'we'?" I queried.

"Oh, several of the lads are asking to come and watch," Evan replied happily.

"Well, you just tell them that once a year is enough for them to laugh at the English." I spluttered as a nasty thought hit me. "My God, you haven't fixed for these horses to be in the Arms Park have you?"

Pictures of the Christians being thrown to the lions in the Colosseum rose before my eyes. Evan assured me that I should be on safer ground than that, and anyway they were not intending to defile the sacred turf with anything as mundane as an equine operation.

I duly arrived at Evan's house at lunch time on an unusually dry and sunny day.

"At least we will not get wet when we cast the horse in the field," I said with some relief.

"Don't worry, you have got a splendid operating theatre awaiting you," he assured me.

After lunch we made tracks for this operating theatre in Evan's car. It transpired that the horse was on a neighbour's farm about twenty miles away. As the great bulk of the distance was along little winding roads which cascaded up and down steep valleys, the journey was like a ride on a roller coaster at a fair ground, except that Evan drives somewhere between Jehu and Stirling Moss.

Just as I was beginning to wonder if my will was in proper order, we turned into a farmyard on the side of a one in four hill. As we pulled up, the farmer, a large broad-shouldered man unlike most of his compatriots, walked over to us.

"Good day, Evan, we are all ready for you."

I was introduced to yet another Davies, who owned the farm and kept a number of fine Welsh Cobs. I shook hands, being careful not to have mine crushed in his enormous fist.

"I believe you have found somewhere for us to cast the horse?" I said.

"Oh doctor, there's a place better than you'd find in Carmarthen hospital," he grinned. "Got a bed soft enough for young Dilys Jones, her that runs that clothes shop in Tregarron, and a lot more besides clothes, so I gather."

While he was disparaging the reputation of one of the local ladies, the owner of my patient came up and introduced himself.

"Pleased to meet you," he said, slapping me on the back, "Evan here has been saying that you can put my old mare right, and that at much less then he would charge."

He gave a wink to Evan and went on to tell me how his old mare was the apple of his eye, carried him hunting twice a week and pulled the fodder cart round the sheep for the rest of the week.

"Terrible puffed she gets with her old wind now. Just you clear her pipes for me and the old girl will see another ten years."

As I learned more about my patient, he led me round the corner to a large shed. I looked inside and saw two aged tractors and various balers and hay turners. As my eyes became accustomed to the gloom I saw that the rear half of the shed was filled with particularly strong smelling silage. Working like ants over the silage were at least eight men and women, who were busy levelling the top of the heap into something resembling a large treacly table. The farmer and the horse owner stood back with some pride at their ingenuity at producing such a good casting bed. Well, it was big enough and certainly soft enough. In fact at my first step onto it, I sunk to my knees. Before I could raise any protest the mare was walked into the shed. Threading her way cautiously through the tractors and other obstacles, she stood placidly at the base of the heap.

Evan had agreed to act as anaesthetist and with no pause he proceed to run the anaesthetic into her vein. Before I could gather my thoughts, she toppled over gently onto the edge of the silage. Immediately at least a dozen willing hands seized on her legs and pulled her to the top of the heap. I rushed forward to put the ropes and hobbles on the horse before she disappeared into the gluey silage. Unfortunately in my rush I tripped and fell flat on my face in the stinking mass. This was as well received as an overture to a Mozart opera by the assembled throng. I managed to fix the hobbles in place and suggested that we turn the mare onto her back. The helpers enthusiastically pulled her legs up and secured her safely so that I could start work at the front end.

As I shaved her throat and gathered up my tools, I suddenly realised that I was slowly losing my patient. Very gently she was sinking through the operating table. I don't think that I have ever carried out an operation with more speed. All went well, but by the time that I had tied the last suture in her neck, she had sunk a good eighteen inches lower and was now completely wedged in the clinging mass of silage.

"What shall we do now?" I looked up questioningly at Evan.

"Don't worry doctor," the farmer shouted, "we will lift her out easy as you like."

With that he started up one of the antique tractors and turned it towards the heap. Lifting up the front rake, he slid the tines through the hobble rope.

"Steady now," he yelled, "let her come."

The rake lifted slowly up, raising the mare with a noise like a cork coming out of a bottle. As she cleared the heap, he backed the tractor and gently deposited the unconscious animal over the silage to the edge. There she was unhitched and the hobbles removed. I gave her a ration of anti-tetanus serum and some antibiotics, which I hoped would counteract whatever little creatures lived in the smelly silage, and told the owner that she should get to her feet within the hour.

I stood back and pondered as to why we had spent so much money on a sophisticated operating theatre and lifting hoist to move our patients at home. We could just have well have bought an old Fergy tractor. While thinking of this, the party led me into the house and washed the majority of the mess from my clothes. Everyone then celebrated their respective performances with several good measures from the bottle. It began to look as though the party was set for the evening at least, so Evan and I made our apologies and left them to it.

The second operation was scheduled for a farm more than forty miles away. At least this was a simple tendon operation and would not involve a general anaesthetic nor the problem of a suitable operating table. We arrived at the farm to be greeted again by what seemed to be a small army of helpers and onlookers. There was a great air of expectancy to see the English surgeon at work. He by now was quite sure that his original thoughts about confining his efforts to his home patch were more than justified. This time the procedures went off without a hitch. So much so that you could feel the general air of disappointment from the spectators. The trouble with the successful tendon surgery is that there is very little to see. No slashing great incisions with arteries pumping blood and arrays of tubes pouring fluid into veins. Just a tiny cut about one inch long and only one final stitch. I kept assuring the audience that it was a very sensitive operation and extremely difficult to perform, but I could judge that they did not feel that they were getting their money's worth.

After bandaging the leg and leaving instructions for the aftercare, we set off back to Evan's house. I apologised for the sense of anticlimax, but he reassured me that it would have increased his stock greatly in the district. Not liking to press him on this rather ambiguous remark, I suggested that he rang the farmer to make sure that our first horse had gone home in one piece. The number rang for a couple of minutes and then I heard obvious sounds of merriment from the other end of the line. I listened as Evan asked if the mare had recovered. I saw him start to laugh, and he put down the receiver.

"Well, Charles, you cannot complain over my part in the operation. She only got up half an hour ago. By then it was too dark to load her into the trailer since the Land Rover has no lights. Anyway poor Mostyn is now on his way home leading his mare across the fields!"

It was certainly a different world from Berkshire, but I decided to confine my surgical attempts to home territory in future. If only I could persuade myself to keep to these sensible decisions. Within a year I was persuaded to try my luck again, but not I am afraid back in Wales. They learn quickly west of Offa's Dyke.

CHAPTER 4
An Irish Idyll (1960's)

Ihave never needed much encouragement to make a visit to Ireland. The humour and the hospitality always far outweigh the knowledge that the problems of assessing the potential of any horse will be clouded more than usual by the constant flow of Irish blarney and unsolicited advice. The apparent willingness of the Irish farmer to adapt his horse's pedigree to your particular requirement is only matched by his stout advocacy of its virtues and his blindness of eye as to its shortcomings. However it is true to say that I have never yet come across one inhabitant of the Emerald Isle who was not master of his animal. Not for them the frantic attempts to ride a nappy horse. To a man or woman the Irish have an uncanny knack of communicating with their charge.

So it was with pleasurable anticipation that I arranged to accompany Piers Belgrave on a trip to see two likely hurdlers. Piers was one of the newer generation of trainers in the practice. Coming from a well-known racing family, he had set up shop in the district the previous year. With only seven horses in the yard he was anxious to increase his string as quickly as possible. Having received an order from a new owner to find a couple of nice young jumpers, he had communicated his requirements to a well-versed dealer near Dublin.

Now, one of the delights of Ireland was the system of telepathy which passed on information as to who was wanting to buy horses, and who had horses and how much they were requiring for what was certain to be the "best horse in Ireland of its type". In a country where it could take you up to a month to get a leaking tap repaired and where it was virtually impossible to find any soul who can tell you the way to any place which you were seeking, it was astonishing to discover this highly efficient bush telegraph.

Within an hour of his call, Piers' telephone began behaving like the switchboard at Scotland Yard. Incessantly for the next three hours calls were made by trainers, breeders and thick brogued farmers from penny-in-the-slot kiosks. From Cork, Tipperary and Wexford, horses were offered that were bred to catch pigeons and fly over houses, such great 'leppers' were they. By the time we met next morning at Heathrow he had a list of seventeen possible purchases, and that was without the ones that Michael Dwyer, his dealer contact, would have for us. With an armful of formbooks and pedigree references the tall spare figure of Piers came hurrying up to me as I waited at the Aer Lingus counter.

"I am sure that we will find something out of this lot," he said in his slow drawl as he handed me the list of aspirants. "They are all supposed to have some ability, although I can't seem to find more than eleven of them to be mentioned in any Raceform."

I took the list and glanced down it as we waited for the plane to be called.

"Ah, I see there are a couple of old friends here at least. I have examined them within the last three weeks. One is a tiny rabbit of a horse with a twisted front foot and the other is blind in one eye and not too sure of his other one."

Looking on down the list I saw that there were a number of animals which were bred well enough to have run at Royal Ascot, but had not yet seen a racecourse. True, they might have grown into horses which were too big for the flat, but Piers was looking for hurdlers which were ready to run now and not in two years time.

As we climbed up into the sky we narrowed the possibles down to three from the total of seventeen. One of these was a well-bred four year old in the stable of a trainer in Cork, the others were in flat race stables near the Curragh and had been placed as three year olds. One of the stables was more of a dealer's yard in that every horse there was always for sale should a customer with the right sort of money come along.

Piers had arranged to meet Michael Dwyer, the agent, at an hotel in Newbridge at mid-day. The plan was to see two or three horses that afternoon and to catch the evening flight back to London. I warned him that from past experience he was trying to fit a great deal into one day. I had found it advisable to allow at least two hours for each visit. This gave time for the welcome, the inspection of the animal, and a bare minimum for the final sales pitch and hospitality. In several cases I have know the latter to continue well into the night. However Piers was full of confidence that he could keep to his schedule. Such is the optimism of the ignorant.

On arrival at Dublin we hurried to the hire car counter. Alas, we discovered after a fevered search of our respective wallets that neither of us could raise a driving licence. Ten minutes of concentrated talk and simulated Irish charm finally overcame the problem. I persuaded the girl behind the counter that I had returned several cars safely on previous visits to her country. Piers foolishly agreed to rely on my knowledge of the road to Newbridge and we set off towards Dublin. The city is one of those through which it always seems easier to find your way by instinct rather than planned thought. On my own I usually manage to find my way about with no great difficulty; however when laden with the responsibility of guiding a third party, I invariably finish up in a one-way street with Phoenix Park looming at the far end like the proverbial end of the rainbow.

On this occasion the rush hour traffic combined with a slight fog brought me to a dead end by the Liffey. As I looked back to reverse out, I noticed to my horror that my stethoscope was missing from the rear seat. I then remembered having left it on the hall table at home where I had put it next to my raceglasses. I broke the news to Piers, who by then was becoming resigned to spending his day in the nethermost parts of Dublin city.

"Not to worry," I said with more confidence than I felt, "I am sure that I can borrow one from a friend."

With that I stopped at the next phone box and rang a colleague in Kildare.

"Sure now, Charles, don't worry at all. I will leave one at the dress shop on the centre of the square in Naas at Auntie Mary's, but mind now it is an Irish stethoscope and you will probably hear the wee folk singing through it. You know that you English love to romance about our strange customs."

A few more minutes driving brought us to the Guinness brewery and I knew at last where I was. We made good speed to Naas where true to his word my friend had left a stethoscope. I picked it up from the well endowed lady, who assured me that it worked for hadn't she just been listening to her own heart with it. My offer to try it again on her chest being refused, I rejoined my companion and we made tracks for Newbridge and Michael Dwyer.

We walked into the bar of the hotel and were greeted by a small, red-faced man with twinkling eyes and a broad smile. He was dressed in a very old tweed suit with highly polished jodphur boots and a large spotted bow tie.

"Piers, my boy," he exclaimed as he came forward with hand outstretched, "how great to see you. I remember when you came over with your uncle to Punchestown as a young lad. Is he well, now - oh such a grand man, and a terrible good judge of a horse. But then I am sure you have taken after him in that. You did right to get in touch with old Michael to find you just the horse that you want."

I was introduced to him, and we shook hands while at the same time he shouted to the landlord for two large jars of scotch.

"Come now and sit down", he said as he ushered us to a table by a roaring fire. "I have found two horses for you, which will suit you fine. Big strong types with plenty of speed and both can be bought well worth the money. One is just up the road at Sean Dwyer's - a decent type who was placed in a bumper at Clonmel last week. Sean is wanting to keep him for Cheltenham, but I told him that Tommy Belgrave's nephew was after buying a horse like him, and Sean said he would be delighted for you to have him. The second lad is over in Wexford, and he is a really great stamp of horse. Second in the Leger and placed in two other Group races, he is certain to win over hurdles for you."

Whilst Michael was rushing enthusiastically onwards, I had a glance at our list. The Leger horse in Wexford was not one of our three possibles, so that meant that we now had four to choose from. We finished our drink and declined a second with Piers protesting that we had a lot to do before our return home. Michael shrugged on his coat and led us out to his car. Still singing the praises of the horses he drove us out past the Curragh racecourse to Sean Dwyer's large ivy-covered house on the edge of the training grounds.

We drove into the yard and Michael scrambled out to find the trainer. As Piers and I stood waiting I heard a voice shout,

"Hello there, Charles, what brings you to the thieves' kitchen?"

I looked around to see Tommy Walls, a trainer from Newmarket, with a tall man and a good looking blonde in a fox fur.

"Hope you are not trying to buy the one we are here to see," he grinned as we introduced each other. "We are looking for a colt to run in decent six or seven furlong races for next year."

He seemed relieved when I explained that we were wanting a jumper.

"You'll be seeing that young chestnut, I expect," he laughed, "John Kimber of the Northern Counties Bloodstock Agency is coming to see him this afternoon."

Before I could remonstrate with him for adding to Sean Dwyer's high pressure salesmanship, Michael beckoned us to go into the house. I followed Piers into the kitchen, where we were introduced by name to the trainer. A small wiry man, he looked as though he had lived all his life in the saddle. His complexion was best described as weather-worn leather and you could swear he had washed in saddle soap since birth.

"What did they say about that three year old?" he asked Piers, gesturing to Tommy and his owners. "He's a grand horse for them. Just a bit stumped up on the hard ground or he'd have won four races for me. But now, you will be wanting to see your fellow - I am a fool to sell him, but I would like you to have a decent horse seeing as you are just starting. He should have won last week, but for that ape of an amateur who rode him. He came wide around the turn at Clonmel and nearly went off up the road instead of turning into the straight. I have schooled him over a hurdle, and by God if he is not a natural jumper, I'll pack the job in!"

With that he led us out to see the animal. Sixteen hands high with a great front, over slightly at the knee and with a frame that would need an extra long girth to fit around him, he certainly looked the part. The lad tacked him up and pulled him out into the yard.

"Give him a trot for us," I asked.

The boy set off up the yard at a brisk pace, As he went I noticed that he dragged his near hind leg very slightly. When he came back to us I saw that there was quite a thickening on his fetlock joint. As he saw me feel the leg, Sean launched off on a story as to how he had hit it in the box some months before when he was being broken.

"Never worried him at all," he assured us with Michael giving an encouraging nod to his companion.

The lad jumped up on the chestnut and we all followed him out to the paddock, where he set off at a fast canter round the edge of the fence. When he passed us for the second time Sean yelled at the rider to pop him over a couple of hurdles in the centre of the field. There was no doubt that he jumped and galloped like a racehorse. We saw him back into the yard, and we all retired to the kitchen for a coffee, while the horse cooled down. Leaving us to finish our coffee and allowing Michael to take up the task of continuing to extol the horse's undoubted ability, the trainer departed off to work on his other victims. After five minutes or so he came back.

"Great people - taken him off me for a thousand more than I expected. They think that Newmarket will suit him better, as he can do all his work on their all-weather gallops. Must be marvellous things, those sort of gallops," he said with a wink at Michael.

We thanked him for our coffee and went back to the stable. The horse was caught up again and brought out to trot up the yard. For the second time he moved unevenly with his hind legs. I turned to Piers and said that he could not buy a lame horse. At this both the Irishmen began a long spiel to the effect that the horse was not what you would call lame.

"Sure, he's a bit cramped on that old joint, but not so you would worry. Hadn't he always been like that and he had run like the Holy Ghost was after him last week with never a thought to his leg."

They went on in this vein for several minutes, but when it became clear that Piers and I were not to be swayed, Sean said,

"Well, never mind then, I've a customer as will buy him this afternoon. Would you ever be interested in an Even Money horse over there?" He pointed to a big black gelding who was weaving backwards and forwards over the stable door.

"He's won three chases this year and he would be a certainty in England, what with his low handicap and being a great ride for any man."

Piers protested that he did not quite fit the bill for his client, so we made our way back to Michael's car. He seemed to accept our dismissal of the horse quite resignedly, and turned his attentions to the virtues of the Leger colt in Wexford as we drove down a back road from Sean's house. As we turned a corner I looked out of the window and to my surprise saw an immaculate all-weather gallop along the road side. No wonder he had winked at his confederate when Tommy had mentioned the Newmarket facilities.

We wound our way over the low hills into Wexford and came on a little village nestled in a hollow. At the far end was a white house with two yards separated by a large hay barn and covered school for exercising the horses. As we pulled up, the head lad came over to meet us. Putting his head through the window, he shook hands with Michael and explained that the guv'nor was up on the gallops, but we were to go into the office and have a jar. Piers and I followed him in and the dealer poured out liberal measures of the trainer's whisky.

"Now this horse will be just what you want," he assured my colleague. "He is the best novice in Ireland and your vet will find nothing wrong with him."

With this assurance we awaited the arrival of Willy Shane, a man whom I had never met, but whose reputation as a shrewd trainer had often been recognised in England. With two Champion Hurdles and a Grand National to his credit he was accepted as a master of his craft. Ten minutes later the great man came hurrying into the office full of apologies for keeping us waiting. Insisting that we have another drink, he began to tell my companion what a sacrifice he was making in letting his horse go to England.

We went out to see this paragon of a hurdler, and as we walked towards his box, I pulled my stethoscope out of my coat pocket.

"Is it a vet that you are?" he questioned hesitantly. I nodded agreement and went forward to listen to the colt's heart.

"Well now, I'll not be trying to mislead you, but you will find that he makes a slight bit of a whisper, not that it is likely to affect his racing."

I thanked him for the information and Piers said that nevertheless he would like to see the horse out. We walked out after the animal to a large grass field with a fairish slope at one end. The stable jockey was riding the colt and he let him canter steadily round in a big circle. I listened carefully and there was no doubt that the horse made a slight whistle when he breathed in. After he had been round three times the trainer suggested that we had heard enough.

"Could we please not see him go a bit faster, preferably up the bank at the lower end of the meadow," I asked. Mumbling something about the bad ground there, Willy told the rider to take him steady up the hill. I had meanwhile run over to the bank so that I could at least be in earshot as he worked across. I need not have bothered to run. As the horse increased his pace, so did the noise of his breathing. When he reached the top he was blowing like a whale.

For the second time that day I shook my head and Michael lost another nice slice of commission. Mr Shane however did not seem to be in any way abashed, and apologised for wasting our time, saying that if he had known a vet was coming he would have saved us a journey. Still, as with Sean Dwyer, he harboured no ill feelings, but instead invited us all into the house for an excellent lunch, lubricated by some very good vintage port. For me it is one of the endearing facets of the Irish character - if one deal falls through, why worry, another will be around the corner. Michael threw off his disappointment, or perhaps the port merely clouded it, as we drove back to Newbridge.

"Never mind, old friend, we will find another for you soon. I know of several more which could be bought worth the money."

We left him at the hotel with the promise that he would soon be back in touch with Piers.

I suggested that we call at my friend's house in Kildare to see if he knew of any possible animals for us. Piers agreed, saying that we had just time to see one more locally before we caught our plane home. We were lucky to catch the vets in the middle of an operation, and they directed us to the trainer who had phoned Piers the previous night. Promising to return, we drove off down the Port Laoise road and turned up into Offaly for about ten miles. The trainer was out when we arrived but his daughter assured us that it would be all right to see the horse in question. She disappeared to fetch the head man and excused herself, saying that she had to catch the post office before it closed. The head man took us to a small whippety-looking bay gelding, which looked as though it would be better suited to a seller at Wolverhampton on the flat rather than a bustling hurdle race at Sandown Park. He fetched his saddle and bridle and jumped up on the little horse's back. When Piers said it looked too small to carry much weight in a jump race, the lad laughed and said he must not be bothered by his looks, he would carry fourteen stone and still win with a cart harnessed on behind him - he was so strong.

We followed as instructed up a rough track and through a yard. Our man continued over a small meadow and trotted between the remains of a broken gate in a wall into another field. We panted on breathlessly behind. As we reached the gateway the lad shouted over his shoulder for us to watch how the 'little divil' could operate. With that he flung the horse off at a fast clip and aimed straight at a stone wall in the corner. The horse certainly gave it a good foot as he landed in the next field and turned sharply round to jump back over a stiffish hedge between two trees. The rider did not pause, but pointed the horse at an old tree trunk which was lying in the field. This he cleared, as well as a six foot ditch on the landing side.

"Come back to us now," shouted Piers, but to no avail. Man and horse aimed themselves at another hedge on the opposite side of the meadow. This time the horse stood right back and hit the top of the hedge hard, dislodging the pilot. The next minute we saw the animal disappearing across the corner of the field towards an open gate out onto the road. The jockey meanwhile picked himself up and shook himself like a dog coming out of water and took off in pursuit.

"Get back to the car," I yelled over my shoulder to Piers. He needed no second bidding and his long legs soon overtook me as we stumbled over the rough ground in the farmyard. We backed the car out and started off in the hope of cutting the horse off. We soon caught up the rider, who jumped into the back seat.

"There now, didn't I tell you he was as strong as an ox," he puffed. "If the old brute would learn to look first, there is no fence in the world that he would touch."

"What on earth were you trying to prove by that extraordinary performance," drawled Piers in an irritated voice. "I didn't want to buy a hunter that was only big enough to carry my boots. All we wanted was to see him gallop. I can get him jumping hurdles at home without an idiot like you ruining him."

"But master," the man answered with a look of some bafflement, "I thought you wanted a show jumper. The guv'nor said I was to leap him over the hedges for the English gentleman when he arrived."

During this explanation we came up on the horse who had found his way into a kale field and was now standing nibbling the nearest stalks. His rider hopped out of the car and caught him with no trouble. Leaving him to walk back, we returned to the stable to find the daughter of the house, who had come back from her visit to the village. We told her what had happened and she apologised as best she could between gales of laughter.

"Well, would you ever believe it," she wailed, "there's me thinking you were the two to see my jumper. Did you not telephone from Limerick to say you would be arriving this afternoon?" She broke off to greet her horse who seemed none the worse for his escapade. Indeed he looked quite pleased with his performance.

"It will be the Royal Buck colt that you were after," she said as she closed the stable door on her horse. "Never mind, I will get him out for you now."

With that she led us to another range of dilapidated boxes and brought out a fine big bay with an intelligent head and great strong limbs.

"Second at the Park last month," she said as she led him out.

"He won a race at Naas last October, but he was disqualified when the jockey dropped his weight cloth going into the scales and forgot to pick up all the lead."

Taking the head man's tack from him, she expertly put it on the big bay and vaulted into the saddle.

"Follow me to the field over the road," she shouted and again we set off in pursuit. This time we entered a large undulating field, and stood by the gate to prevent any further mishaps. With a good hold on him the girl let him stride on past us and turned at the end of the field to let him come back at a good half speed gallop. Not only was he a good mover but he looked fit and well. I commented on this when she pulled up by us, and she said that of course he was fit since her father planned to run him at Mallow in a couple of days.

After another hour, three cups of tea, and a potted history of her life and that of her family, we got back into the car with Piers determined to buy the gelding. Father had gone to market and no amount of phone calls had succeeded in tracking him down. We now knew the horse, his breeding and his form, which incidentally read better than we had hoped. The only item missing was the price tag, and no amount of persuasion was going to drag even an indication from the daughter. So the unfortunate Piers was left to sweat on this until he got home that evening and could telephone the trainer.

The thought of that turned our attention to the clock. By then it was half past five and we were nearly seventy miles from our aeroplane, which was due to take off in an hour.

"I did say that you had cut things a bit fine," I grinned, "we are nearly as close to your 'bumper' horse in Tipperary as we are to Dublin. Why don't we put up somewhere for the night and see him early next morning? We can then catch a plane back from Cork to London." Piers looked doubtfully at me.

"I don't know that I ought not to get back tonight. I was planning to school two horses tomorrow on Mann Down with Bill Makepeace's jockey. Still I suppose it is silly not to see the other horse now that we are so near."

The plan having been hatched, I stopped at the next telephone kiosk and called another of my chums in Tipperary. I asked him to book us two rooms at a local hotel and then to bring his wife down to dine with us.

"Absolutely not Charles," he answered. " I won't hear of it. You are both to come and stay with us for the night, see your horse in the morning and then stay and have a day with the hounds."

I thanked him for this generous offer, which I gladly accepted even though previous experience of his hospitality should have sounded a note of caution. I declined the offer of a day's hunting, since even if Piers could cancel his schooling session I knew that I would have a lot of work to catch up on when I got back to the practice.

We got to my friend's house and the usual boisterous Irish reception, with the result that several times that evening I wondered whether I had done the right thing in suggesting that we stayed on. By next morning when I awoke to hammer blows in my head, I knew full well that we had made a strategic error. During the evening Piers made contact with the trainer in Offaly and managed to buy the horse after agreeing to meet him some way on the price. In fact I believe that they were about three thousand pounds apart at the beginning of the bargaining. The trainer came down five hundred pounds with my companion climbing the remaining necessary two and a half thousand. Not quite a fifty fifty shift, but with a shrewd horse dealer it was probably the best that could be done. Piers had also managed to contact Seamus O'Reilly, the owner of the bumper horse in Tipperary, to arrange that we would see his four year old horse at nine o'clock next morning.

As day dawned, my host banged on the door at an ungodly hour and summoned me out to see his foals in the paddocks. I have seldom felt less like viewing high spirited youngsters, as it was all I could do to focus on my next footstep. With throbbing head I tried to elicit some enthusiasm for a bunch of colts, all bred in the purple and worth a king's ransom. I queried as to how he could sleep so easily in bed with so many valuable animals cavorting about in what at that time were not very safely fenced paddocks. He laughed and replied that he never had a worry for "surely didn't the bank own all of them". He had started buying expensive stock some few years before with no money, only what a kindly bank manager had lent him. As things were to turn out, the manager was not only kind but extremely far-seeing, since the enterprise was to prove most profitable.

Following breakfast, for my part consisting of very strong black coffee, we set off with me leaving Piers to do the navigating. Neither of us said a lot, the effort of speech was beyond our fuddled minds. We got to the square in Fermoy at a quarter to nine, where we were to meet Mr O'Reilly. As we were early I suggested that we go and find another cup of black coffee to try and revive ourselves. We had only just emerged from the car when a very battered old Ford drew up and the driver gave a blast on the horn. Leaning out of his window he asked,

"Would you be the English gentlemen who are looking to buy a horse?"

Piers nodded agreement and Mr O'Reilly crawled from his car, resembling for all the world a caterpillar shrugging off an out-grown skin.

He was an immense man, weighing at a guess some twenty stone. He took off an old trilby hat to reveal half a dozen wispy hairs attempting to cover his head. His clothes could only be said to match his car. They had obviously done many years service and at a guess had been purchased when Mr O'Reilly was but a shadow of his present bulk. String had replaced buttons in all the vital areas, and the pockets waved like semaphore flags in the slight breeze. We explained our immediate need of coffee, but he waved this aside,

"Follow me," he ordered. "Mother will have a strong pot of something brewing on the hob for you. I will lead the way for you are sure to get lost." So saying he squeezed into the driving seat and the car coughed into action, while we returned to our car and prepared to follow our leader. He led us round every tiny lane in Tipperary, or so it seemed, before he eventually turned into a rough little yard alongside a house which gave the impression of being propped up against the bank for survival.

We went after him into the house, Piers having to duck his head by a good foot. We were introduced to Mother, a cheerful soul, who despite her ample frame looked small beside her man.

"Will you fetch a hot drink for the gentlemen, Mother," said Seamus, "I'll get a drop of the hard stuff to warm them up."

With one voice we declined this kind offer, and settled for a steaming cup of Mother's hot stuff.

"So you are after seeing my Patrick, are you. A fine sort he is, fast as a stag and without a whisper of the devil in him."

We asked how he had come by such a well-bred horse, since it did not look as though he could afford to buy a donkey, let along a decent racehorse.

"Well," he grinned, "he was a bit of a handful as a two year old, kept burying his jockeys until they had all had enough of him. I met the owner one day at Ballsbridge Sale and he offered him to me cheap to get the horse off his hands. I brought him home and we very soon fixed him. Tied him to the shafts of an old cart and let him play. Jaysus, but he kicked the divil out of the cart for two days, and them I put him on the hay rake. Didn't he go round the hay fields like as though he was coming into the last bend at Leopardstown, but that cured the monkey. I drove him round the farm and rode him to round up the cattle all that winter till he rode like a lady's hack. You will understand that with me on his back he could not even raise the show of a buck. I took him to Kerry in a bumper race to let him have a look at a racecourse, and then gave him an easy race at Mallow last fortnight. Sure, he is a certainty next week at Listowel if I decide to loose him off."

With this potted history of Patrick's Lament, the proud owner took us out into the yard. We picked our way through puddles and year old heaps of straw and cow dung. I was not surprised that Michael Dwyer had not found this horse, he with his highly polished footwear. He led us past the stables which in the main lacked a roof, and pulled open the door of what could only be a pig sty. Stepping over a broken concrete trough, he pulled back the top door of the living accommodation. The lintel was not more than five feet from the ground, and we both had to stoop to follow him into the box. It took a minute for my eyes to get used to the gloom, but then I saw a large grey head peering inquisitively forward at me. Seamus put a halter over the horse's head and, beckoning us to move back, led out his pride and joy. Well might he be proud of him. Even as the horse almost knelt down to scrape under the lintel, you could see that he was chock full of quality. When he emerged into daylight he stood a good sixteen and a half hands high with great length of rein and powerful quarters.

"Would you like to climb on him?" he questioned me. Neither of us felt up to the responsibility of steering his valued horse round the adjoining fields, certainly not after hearing how he had performed in his last home.

"Never mind, I will give him a spin for you," said Seamus.

Piers held him while the farmer went to collect his gear, and I had a quick look over the animal. Once saddled the horse walked over to a low wall in the yard and waited for his rider to get aboard and lower himself into the saddle. Then off he set at a brisk trot to a track up through the wood. We cut through a path and met them in a ploughed field behind the trees.

"Stay still," shouted Seamus, " and I will give him a blow for you to hear."

With that he urged the gelding into a fair gallop across the furrows. Like a cat, the horse sped from one furrow to the next as though he was gifted with wings and not hooves.

"He will do," said Piers in an awestruck voice. I could only agree with him, for he was a magnificent sight. I finished my examination while my companion went indoors to try and clinch the deal. By the time I returned to report that all was well, he had already bought the horse and was fixing up transport back to England.

"You will be wanting some luck money," chuckled Seamus. "Here Mother, fetch that parcel from the larder. The one I brought home last night."

Mother disappeared and came back with a large paper parcel containing what looked uncommonly like a brace of salmon trout. Piers took the package and we wished him good-bye, making our way to the car.

Our next problem was to find our way back to Cork airport. Fortunately in our now more sober state of mind this did not prove too difficult. It was therefore two elated people who boarded the first flight to London. I wished Piers good luck with his purchases as we shared the fish in the car park and made my way back to Lambourn and normality. The two horses were to prove well worth the journey, since between them they won Piers' owners seven races, the lad from Cork graduating to be a successful steeplechaser around the park courses of London.

CHAPTER 5
A Call to Cologne (1960's)

Work for bloodstock agents tended to be spasmodic, but usually urgent. An order is received for a certain horse and there is a mad rush to have it examined, sold and delivered as soon as possible. The export trade in horses in the late 1960's was brisk. So it was when John Kimber of the Northern Counties Bloodstock phoned me one evening.

"Charles, can you get to Newmarket tomorrow to see a two year old, which I want to buy for a German client. I have got the horse booked on a flight at the end of the week."

"Steady on," I answered, "I can't possibly do it tomorrow. I will try and get up there the next day, only I must be back in Lambourn by evening stables."

I asked him what the horse was and what his client expected it to do in Germany. It was called All Souls and had won three races that season. It was bred to stay at least a mile and the prospective owner hoped to win on the flat with it and then to send it hurdle racing.

As I went to put the phone down I heard John speak again.

"Oh, I forgot to tell you that apparently, the horse has had an accident to one of his front legs. His trainer says that it does not affect him now."

As usual there was a catch, these jobs rarely seemed to be completely straightforward. Anyway I promised to get in touch with Michael Craze, the trainer.

I phoned Craze right away and arranged to see All Souls at first lot in a couple of days (first lot is when the horses are taken out for exercise, which can be at any time between six o'clock and eight o'clock in the morning). Craze warned me that the horse had been out of training for the last three or four weeks, since the flat racing season had finished. However, he was sure that he would be fit enough to do a good canter.

A Call to Cologne

The alarm clock rang at four o'clock in the morning, and once again I vowed to change my profession. As I struggled to my feet, I began to mutter curses on J. Kimber and then on all bloodstock agents. As usual, Wendy told me to shut up and let her sleep, and why had I agreed to do the job if I was so busy. I went downstairs to make a cup of tea and pondered over her question. Why did I take on these errands? We had more than enough to do in our own parish without gadding about the country like peripatetic bees. It wasn't as though I even liked travelling. It must have been something to do with my lack of ability to say no, coupled with some strange egotistical pride in the fact that an outsider had actually asked me in preference to numerous other practitioners. The truth lay somewhere between the fact that, as a practice, we were known to be fairly prompt and obliging and the fact that we were possible cheaper than a lot of others.

Dismissing these philosophical thoughts from my mind, I started up the car and began the cross-country route of more than one hundred miles to Newmarket. I arrived in good time, since more normal people were still in their beds and there was next to no traffic on the roads. I knocked on Craze's door and was ushered into the kitchen, where the trainer and his assistant were getting outside steaming cups of tea.

"You made good time," Craze said with a smile, "have a cup. Your horse is all ready for you. Did Mr Kimber explain about his leg?"

I nodded and said that he had just mentioned that the gelding had met with a slight accident, but that it had now recovered.

"I don't know about a slight accident," Craze laughed, "he nearly skinned the whole of his ruddy leg. It took three months to heal up, and right in the middle of the season when he should have won more races. As it was I could only train him again in September and we just gave him one more run at the back end when he came fourth in a nursery."

"How did he do it?" I asked, gratefully gulping down the hot milky tea.

"Caught his leg in a hay net and hung there most of the night. Bloody fool of a kid failed to tie up the net properly, and he is the sort of horse who is always playing about in his box anyway. The head lad found him in the morning with his fetlock through the net and the skin rolled down from his knee to his fetlock. Thank God it did not do any real damage. Anyway you will see for yourself. William here will show you the horse and take you out to the gallops. Do what you like with him, but remember that I have not worked him since he last ran."

With that the assistant trainer picked up his cap and held the door open for me. He took me round to the stables and led me into All Souls' box. I noticed that his hay was in a neat pile on the floor, no second chances with a net. He was a well-developed chestnut with a plain head and flashing white eye. Just the type to be a bit hot, I thought to myself. Talking to him, I approached to listen to his heart and feel his legs.

"He is quite quiet," the assistant said reassuringly, "only he eats vets for breakfast."

This was an old ploy, and usually meant that the animal was as docile as a sheep, but the young lads would always try it on for a new vet or a blacksmith.

All Souls was pulled out and joined by the stable hack for company and a lead up to the sand gallop. I got into William's car and we bumped over the grass to a spot about four furlongs from the bottom of the strip. The two horses turned onto the sand and the old hack took a great pull at his lad. He bounded along swinging his head from side to side, obviously enjoying the chance to show off to his young companion. By the time they reached our vantage point the hack was pulling himself up and All Souls was in danger of galloping into his heels.

"Push the old bastard on a bit Joe," William yelled to the rider of the hack. The boy gave him a couple of belts in his side with his rubber boots and the old horse cocked his jaw and accelerated off.

"Whoah up," he shouted to my horse's jockey. The latter applied the brakes and All Souls slowed to a trot, wheeled round and came back to me, blowing from the unexpected exertion. After I had checked his breathing and circulation, I looked round for William.

"OK?" he questioned. "If so, he can walk home. You had better jump in with me and we will see if we can stop the hack."

I glanced up the hill to see the rear end of the horse with rug flapping and the back view of the boy unavailingly hauling at the reins.

"Not to worry, he always stops when he has had enough," the assistant grinned, "but he will probably drop young Peter as he does. He is a past master at whipping round and dropping his shoulder to deposit the apprentices in the dust. The boss used him to give the boys a ride in races for a time, but he had to give up when he lost three jockeys in a row on the way to the start."

We gave pursuit up the side of the sand and topping the brow of the hill, sure enough there was the cunning old devil picking grass with his boy rubbing his shoulder some yards away.

"All right, Peter?" questioned William. The answer was a dubious affirmative, but the injury was more to pride than to body. We caught the hack and reloaded Peter on board, leaving the horse to bring him home for breakfast.

Once back at the stable I rejoined my animal. I ran my hand down his off foreleg. There was a thick scar down the front of the leg. The wound had curled round over the tendons above the fetlock, but fortunately had missed the tendons themselves or his racing days would certainly have been ended. As it was, apart from an unsightly scar, there was no reason why his racing career should be further interrupted. I reported to Craze that as far as I was concerned All Souls was in order and could find further glory in Germany. After a good healthy trainer's breakfast I returned down the well-trodden road back to Lambourn. Back at the surgery I telephoned John Kimber with the good news, dictated the certificate, and went back to work.

It was a month later when I had a long distance call from South Africa. Behind the crackle and hiss of the line I could hear John Kimber's voice.

"Charles, is that you? Can you hear me? Now we are in a spot of trouble. I have had a call from my office to say that the Germans are not happy with the horse you vetted for me in Newmarket. I don't know what their worry is, but I understand that it is something to do with a leg. I am stuck out here for a week at the yearling sales, so could you ring my secretary and fix up to go and see the horse again?"

I agreed that I should do this, but any further enquiries were cut short as some operator between Natal and Lambourn pulled out the plug. I could not fathom this out at all. I had no worries about having passed All Souls as fit for racing; true he had not run for a while before I saw him, but his legs seemed fine except for the nasty scar which I had mentioned on my certificate.

I telephoned John's secretary to ask her for more details.

"I don't really know any more than I told Mr Kimber," she replied. "All I have is an irate agent on the line from Frankfurt saying that we sent him an unsound horse and he wants to return it. I stalled him off by telling him that I was sure that Mr Kimber would get you to sort out the problem with him."

I thanked her very much for landing me to deal with an angry German, but then supposing that if it was wrong it must have been my fault, I agreed to talk to the agent. The girl on the phone said she would fix everything with the Germans if I could let her know when I could go over to see the horse. I looked at my diary and agreed to travel over in a couple of days. The sooner the better, since I knew that I should be uneasy until I had got to the bottom of the problem.

A Call to Cologne

The secretary left a message in a couple of hours to say that she had booked me on a Lufthansa flight for Thursday morning to Cologne and that I would be met by the agent, Herr Fleischer. I told our secretary to get some German money from the bank and to phone the English agent's office to warn the Germans that I would arrive at the airport carrying a stethoscope. This was my usual ploy when meeting a stranger. It certainly picked me out from my fellow travellers, and had the added advantage that officials in all countries tend to be favourably inclined to members of what they take to be the medical profession. The only exception to this rule was Saudi Arabia, where the officials showed no tendency to be favourably disposed to any travellers.

I duly caught the flight to Cologne without any hassle, and arrived on time at the airport. It was my first visit to Germany and their reputation for efficiency lived up to its first test. I went through the customs and out into the arrival hall, waving my badge of office in my hand. A tall austere looking man in rimless glasses and a black Homberg and heavy blue overcoat walked towards me.

"Doktor Frank, am I correct?" he said questioningly in a heavily accented voice. I resisted the temptation to extend my hand, doff my hat and say, "Herr Livingston, I presume." His expression did not encourage pleasantries other than a brief smile and a "Good morning".

"Come to my car, please, we go to stables now," he said turning towards the exit.

As I pushed through the swing door, I was met by a blast of freezing air. It had been wet in England, but Cologne was sprinkled with snow, which curled about the road in a stiff breeze. I buttoned up my coat and with spirits decidedly heading towards a low to equal the weather, I followed my guide to a black Mercedes.

"We go twenty kilometres to stables," he volunteered as I settled into the passenger seat.

"Can you tell me what the complaint is with the horse?" I asked.

"I know nothing," he said as he pulled away from the parking area, "I had a call from the owner in Berlin, and he told me that his trainer had said that the horse was no good and could not be trained."

Further enquiries brought out no more information of value, except the fact that the trainer of the stables in Cologne was away on holiday and the head man was in charge. It seemed that the trainer had seen the horse when it arrived from England, and had made no complaint at the time. The trouble only began when he left on leave.

We sped along the monotonous motorway, which was my first look at one of the famous autobahns. Past the ubiquitous tower blocks, we threaded our way along the fast lane, with my companion offering nothing in the way of conversation. I had asked if he spoke much English and explained that my German was limited to about ten words that I had picked up while skiing in Austria and were probably unrepeatable and certainly not apposite for the job in hand. He told me that his English was good, but refrained from giving me any proof of this claim. In fact in the business of small talk he was a clear loser.

Twenty minutes later we came up to a racecourse on our left, and Herr Fleischer slowed down. We turned into a well-wired gateway with security guards posted in a hut from where they flagged us down. A few brief words, which included something about an "Englischer Doktor", and we were through. The stable area was utilitarian in the extreme. Concrete pathways divided up severe office blocks and one storey buildings, which appeared to house the racecourse staff and administration. We drove around the side of what must have been a trial and training track to the stables. This consisted of about six one level buildings, each with a central passage with boxes down each side. The little paint which had been applied to the doors and windows was peeling off, and try as I did, I could not stop my mind from veering on to thoughts of Oflags and Stalags which were still being regularly featured on our television screens. We pulled up outside one of the blocks and I followed my companion through the door.

Inside were several men hurrying about with brooms and forks, and the stables seemed to be full of heavily rugged horses. A short man in riding breeches and brown boots came up to greet the agent. Running his hand through his black sleek hair he spoke in what even to me seemed apologetic tones. Waving his hands in a helpless fashion he pointed at me, the doorway, and the vague direction of the horses. For the first time in my life, but not I was to discover the last, I stood amongst a throng of people having not the remotest idea about what they were saying. I knew that I was figuring in the conversation to at least some extent by the glances that kept shooting my way, but whether to my benefit or detriment I was completely ignorant. The way everything had gone so far, I strongly suspected the latter.

After further discussion, Herr Fleischer turned to me.

"Doktor, I am afraid that we must wait. Follow me, we will drink some coffee."

In vain did I ask if we could not just have a look at the horse first as I was becoming impatient to find out the cause of the complaint, but it was clear that the reception committee was not yet complete. So feeling more and more like a condemned prisoner going to his last meal, I walked back to the car. The still silent Fleischer dropped into his seat and drove slowly back towards the offices. We passed one block and then turned down a narrow alley to pull up outside a room with a glass door, which was steamed up from the heat inside. My companion opened the door and I entered what I took to be the stable lads canteen.

We sat at a small table with an oilskin cloth, covered with the stains of countless cups and glasses. The grey haired lady behind the counter carried round two small cups of black coffee, which she dumped onto our table producing two more stains to add to the collection. It began to look as though attack was going to be my best line of approach, as the hospitality was noticeable for its total lack of friendliness.

"What the hell is going on, Herr Fleischer," I asked and not giving him time to reply, I went on, "I have come all this way from England to see a horse which you say must be returned and I am not even allowed to look at it. The trainer is not here and I presume the owner is in Berlin still, although as he probably knows nothing about horses anyway, that will not matter too much."

He was obviously taken aback by my evidently irritable remarks, but he allowed himself a weak smile from what was probably his ration of five or six a day.

"I am very sorry Doktor, I have been rude but I am a worried man. If the horse goes back to England I shall lose my commission and maybe my customer. You are correct about the owner. He is a very rich businessman, who has many horses both here and in Munich. I am his advisor but there are many in Germany who would like to replace me. It is sad that Emil Braun, the trainer here, is away since he is a sensible man and truthful to deal with. Instead we have to see the trainer from Munich who is coming especially to see you. He has ordered that we do not see the horse until he arrives."

"So that is the reason why the head man looked so unhappy," I said beginning to understand the intrigue.

"Yes, I am afraid there is no liking between the men in Cologne and those in Munich, only great jealousy," he answered with a heavy shrug.

We finished our coffee and returned to the car.

"We will see if they have arrived," Herr Fleischer said, using up yet another of his meagre ration of smiles. As we drove round the corner to the stable, I noticed a large car had been parked by the doorway, and three or four men in heavy overcoats with fur lined collars stood in a knot in the entrance. We climbed out and the agent shook hands with the newcomers, turning to introduce me.

The Munich trainer was a large heavily built man, shrouded in an expensive coat and large fur hat which came down almost to his eyes. He shook hands and looked me over as one would a joint of beef in a butcher's shop. I could not decide from his manner whether he had decided that I was fit for purchase or better left hanging on the hook. However he turned to his companions and made a perfunctory introduction to the taller of the two men, whose name was something like Wurstburger and who did not appear to be involved in the present operation. The third man was stout and round-faced with a bristling grey moustache and metal rimmed half glasses. It struck me that his face rang a distant bell.

"Herr doktor Gruber is our stable veterinarian," Fleischer explained as the doktor held out a limp hand.

Of course, the bell rang again, I had met Gruber at a conference in England some years before. I stepped forward to greet this faintly familiar face, pleased to meet someone with whom I could speak the same language as a fellow practitioner.

"*Gut morgen,*" he replied, "*nein sprichter Englisch.*"

This was strange to say the least, since I could have sworn that we had discussed various treatments for racehorses when we last met.

The larger man nodded to the head man who was standing apprehensively in the background.

"We will now see the horse," he growled.

The procession thus made its way down the passage with Fleischer and Gruber in the rear. The lad stopped at a box halfway down on the left hand side and opened the door. There was All Souls unconcernedly pulling hay from the rack in the far corner of his stable. The lad untied him and a second man ducked under my arm to take off the heavy bandages which shrouded his forelegs. Once he had removed these I stepped forward to feel the offending limbs. I gave a silent sigh of relief - they were both as cold as ice with the tendons standing out, firm as steel bars. I picked up one leg and then the other, squeezing each structure with increasing firmness as my confidence grew - not a single flinch could I detect.

I stood back and looked for Fleischer, who was by this time hiding by the doorpost.

"Well, Herr Fleischer, I can see absolutely nothing wrong with his legs except for that scar tissue down the front, which will never affect him."

Fleischer began to interpret my comments to the trainer and Dr Gruber; however, it seemed that their lack of English did not preclude them from understanding the spoken word. Gruber was pushed forward by the big man, who said something that sounded unpleasant in German. The German vet ran his hands down the legs and pointed unhappily to the thickened scar on the front of the cannon bone. So that was what they were trying to return the horse for - they would have to do a lot better than that.

"Can we please see him trot out in the yard to see if he is lame," I asked Fleischer.

In answer he waved to the lad to bring out All Souls. He took him up the concrete at a smart trot, and as he passed me on his return he gave me a quick grin.

"Perhaps we should see him ridden as he is not the slightest bit lame here."

This was not greeted with any enthusiasm at all, both the trainer and the vet shook their heads saying that the snow had made it impossible for any horse to work.

The animal was lead back into this stable and I caught Gruber by the arm and dragged him back into the yard.

"You know that that old wound will not worry him and there is nothing else wrong with his legs. Why do you think he will not be able to race?"

The doktor shuffled uncomfortably and said something in German that was to the effect that he was sorry not to agree with me but I should understand. With that he was reclaimed by the trainer who grunted a remark at me and regained his car with the tall silent man, who had not to my knowledge spoken a single word. The vet waved his arm at me and hurried to his car which was parked further up the yard.

I turned to Herr Fleischer who was shrugging his shoulders in bewilderment to the head man.

"Come doktor, I believe you do not want to see more," he said. With that he held open the car door for me and we drove off, waving again to the security guards.

"What do you think," he asked as we turned onto the main road, "can he be trained?"

"Of course he can," I answered with a grin. "There is no way that I can advise Mr Kimber to take back the horse. Either the local vet is badly mistaken or it is all a cooked-up story."

"I think that you are right," Fleischer sighed, "I am sure that Emil would never have let this happen. The head man is pleased with the horse, you know."

"I suspected as much when he led the horse out and grinned at me," I answered. "What then is it all about?"

The agent sighed again.

"I believe that that man wants to have the horse in Munich to train himself. He has told the owner that the horse will not stand training in Cologne next season. Now that he cannot return the horse he will try to get it off Emil. The vet is a weak man and he is afraid to upset the owner. The other man is a bloodstock agent from the south and he would be pleased to say that my purchase is no good."

Altogether this looked like a sorry tale, I thought, but I wished that they had not embroiled me in their nefarious scheme. I looked at my watch. It was half past eleven German time. No wonder that I was feeling mighty hungry. Fleischer glanced over at me.

"Doktor, can I drop you at the airport? I believe that there is a plane to London from Bonn at one o'clock. I have to go back to my office to try and speak with Emil."

I fell in with this plan. I might just as well get back home, since my companion had relapsed again into an aggrieved silence, and it did not seem that he was going to provide stimulating company. Herr Fleischer pulled up outside the airport and I picked up my bag off the back seat. As I said goodbye he looked at me.

"I suppose you could not recommend that Mr Kimber takes the horse back to England?"

When I signified that I had not the least intention of falling in with his request, he gave a shrug and with a downcast look he said,

"I was afraid you would refuse, you English are too correct. Now I will have to persuade the owner to leave the horse with Emil."

With that parting shot he drove off, leaving me to find my plane home. The information girl was very helpful, but no – there would be no flight to England before six o'clock, the snow had disturbed the timetable. There was nothing to do but to sit and wait. The restaurant was closed, as seemed to be the norm for all airports except when one had no intention of making use of them. The bookstall had a plentiful supply of literature, but all in German. Not a single thing to read in the English language, and nearly six hours to kill. I collected a bun from the automatic machine and sat down to write my report. These two operations filled precisely seventeen minutes. During the remaining five and a half hours I examined every single article in the departure lounge, even reading each place name on the map of the Ruhr district. By the time my plane was eventually called I was completely numb. I walked like some starved zombie to the plane. The coffee and biscuits were the best sustenance which I had ever tasted. I made a mental note never to criticise airline food again. A resolution that I am afraid has long since gone by the board.

The next morning I phoned Kimber's office and spoke to the secretary. I told her the sorry story and could actually feel her pleasure at the other end of the line.

"I will speak to Mr Kimber later today. He will be relieved at the satisfactory outcome."

Satisfactory – well I didn't know whether I would in reality call my journey to the land of Beethoven and Wagner that. At least Kimber and I were in the clear, but the future for the horse was less obvious. John Kimber rang me that evening and I explained again what had transpired.

"I am so grateful for your help, Charles," he said, "I hope that Herr Fleischer looked after you well."

I told him that he done that which was necessary, but that I had the feeling that he would not be in the market for more horses for a while.

Six months or so later I noticed a paragraph in The Sporting Life about racing in Baden-Baden. A hurdle race there had been won by a horse call All Souls, trained in Munich. So the wretched man had triumphed in the end, and the unfortunate Emil had lost his horse, and presumably Fleischer had lost his client. A sad ending to an unpleasant visit, although at least the horse had come up trumps, and honour at home was satisfied.

CHAPTER 6
A Californian Caper (1970's)

In the everlasting hope that I could learn more, even at my advanced age, I paid a number of visits to varying veterinary conferences. Thus it was that in 1972 I found myself gathered at Terminal 3 of London's Heathrow airport together with around twenty other vets and their respective wives...

We were bound for Los Angeles on a pre-conference trip to savour the delights of the sun, leaving behind a cold November morning. My companions ranged from a respected past president of the Royal College of Veterinary Surgeons to a couple of earnest looking students. How first impressions can lead one astray, especially when launched on a night out in San Francisco! A few drinks and some hectic dancing brought several personality changes!

The party included a jovial Italian whom I was to meet again on a journey to Milan. Only two of the party were previously known to me personally. One was a lugubrious fellow, whom I knew from past experience would use at least five words when two would suffice. His wife on the contrary was one of those delightful people who give the feeling that life is indeed for living. The other acquaintance was a vet from Northern England, whom I had met at previous conferences, like myself struggling to improve his knowledge. He was accompanied by a dour Scotsman, whom I knew only by name. Neither at the airport nor on the plane did he venture any comment at all. This despite an exceptional aeroplane meal, put on to remind us that we were travelling on an American aircraft on Thanksgiving Day.

The plan of the tour was to spend ten days seeing the West Coast and gradually make our way to San Francisco and the conference of the American Equine Practitioners. It was to be my first visit to the West Coast of the USA so Los Angeles with Hollywood and Disneyland were enticing prospects. Sure, I pretended to my colleagues that my prime interest was the surgeries and equine hospitals of our friends in

California although it was to be a holiday for me from veterinary life. We duly arrived, dishevelled and exhausted, in the airport of LA. As usual we queued up to be grilled by the immigration authorities and asked why we had come and had we any intention of murdering the President. Somehow we all managed to convince them that our chief intention was to have a good time and to spend plenty of dollars. The first day we were loaded onto a bus and driven around the delights of Sunset Boulevard with its delicatessens and second hand car lots. The bus driver then treated us to a guided tour around the homes of the stars, even reversing the bus so that we could get a good look at one well-known television comedienne washing her smalls at a kitchen window. Well, I was prepared to believe him, since I could not see anybody at any of the windows, and anyway had I done so I would not have recognised the well-known star.

On my return to the hotel I was summoned to the reception desk to receive an urgent telephone message from England. Fearing the worst, I dialled the number and was connected to a good friend of mine, who at that time was riding over fences as an amateur.

"Charles," he said, "I apologise for interrupting your scientific deliberations, but can you meet me in two days time in Calgary? I have been asked to view a stud of racehorses, which a friend of mine is thinking of buying. I would appreciate it if you could give the animals a good look."

I gave an audible sigh at the thought of my tour being cut short. This was obviously heard over the transatlantic line, as my friend became very apologetic and explained that I would of course be paid for my trouble. The idea of seeing yet another new country overcame my misgivings and I agreed to try and find a plane to take me to Canada to meet him. Having explained my predicament to the tour operator, he was able to give me the destinations at which my colleagues would be staying so that I could rejoin them. A call to a travel agent resulted in my booking on a plane at three o'clock in the afternoon in two days time to Calgary via Seattle.

The next day we were invited to lunch with a vet who had a ranch just outside LA. This was enlivened at the start by my northern vet friend, who provided an unscheduled entertainment for us. The host and his family lived in a typical ranch house. As we entered from the patio, we saw that the whole family was lined up in the front room to greet us. Between us and the welcoming party was an expanse of what my friend took to be a fine blue carpet. With hand outstretched he strode onto the carpet, only to find that rather than Axminster or Wilton it was wet and quite deep. Fishing him out of the pool in his now bedraggled suit, the ladies of the party whisked him upstairs, dried him and kitted him out in the most fashionable cowboy outfit. He may have disturbed the water, but as a method of breaking the ice it was unbeatable.

After a very good lunch and a guided tour around the Arabian horses, which our host bred, we were taken to an equine hospital. This was somewhat of an eye-opener, since at that time such specialist hospitals were limited to around three sites at home, and our own equine clinic relied on a straw bedded barn and a dedicated staff to carry out such limited orthopaedic operations as were possible without too much expensive equipment. The Californian set-up consisted of two operation rooms, of which many a national health unit at home would have been proud. The major source of cases were fractures of the knee joints, an injury which was mercifully rare in the UK. Clearly the difference between American racing on dirt tracks account for the variation in injuries between the two countries.

Our next port of call was away out in the Californian desert, where we were to be entertained by a charming practitioner and his glamorous wife. The latter added to her natural charm by having the great luck to be called Mary Lou. It had long been one of my hopes that I would actually meet somebody with such a romantic name. I had some years before been star-struck by a lady from South Carolina with the true Southern drawl. I was then so entranced that I got carried away to the extent that I spent most of the dinner regaling her with the current strength of the UK economy (of which I really knew very little). Her husband was very obviously not so impressed with my financial expertise. Only after dinner did I learn that he was head of one of the biggest banks in America. It was a good lesson that in future I should stick to dissertations on subjects nearer to my limited field.

To return to our veterinary host. He was in the process of building himself a new hospital, which to my relief was more of a practical nature and one which we could well copy without running into enormous debt. He showed us around the area, which was in the hands of developers, who were about to build a number of expensive residences. These would undoubtedly provide our friend with a ready supply of well-endowed new clients. Typically the developers had decided that before embarking on the dwellings, they should lay out at least two golf courses with resplendent club houses along with tennis courts and swimming pools. He showed us the projected site for the Three Day Event cross country course for the next Olympic Games. It crossed my mind that I should try and persuade someone to invite me as an official at the Games. Unfortunately it would be some years before this came about, and the situation for those games was not quite so idyllic. Regretfully leaving this paradise we made our way back to our hotel, winding through the eight-lane roads leading into Los Angeles. I was relieved that I would not have to drive myself through such a maze of traffic, which made our modern motorways seem like country tracks.

The next morning I could scarcely contain my impatience to see Anaheim and Disneyland. It was indeed all that I had hoped for. The main problem being to decide which of the sites to visit. Whilst making my way to the magic castle I passed a river boat on which I saw my wordy colleague standing on the foredeck. This was not so unusual a sight in itself, but he was adorned in a large Texan hat self-consciously licking a large ice cream. Seeing me on the bank, he thrust the latter into his pocket; an act which did little to improve his smart city suit that he had decided marked him down as a reluctant visitor to such a frivolous place.

After a morning spent in the company of Mickey Mouse and his consort I reluctantly left my colleagues to make my way back to the airport. Clutching my luggage, I found the plane to Seattle and as we climbed through the smog of southern California I looked longingly at the sun-drenched scenery and prepared to re-enter the world of reality once more. How mistaken I was to think that Calgary in December was by any English standards normal. The first thing to strike me was that I might be singularly ill-equipped to face the elements in my light weight summer clothing. The temperature in California had never been less than eighty degrees, whereas Calgary was shivering in temperatures of minus fifteen. I made my way to the appointed rendez-vous at a comfortable and thankfully warm hotel. There I soon found my friend, who introduced me to the attorney dealing with the estate where the horses were lodged. A good meal and wine encouraged me to enquire as to the extent of the projected deal. I gathered that we were to see some twenty horses next day, ranging from broodmares to yearlings and foals. The owner had recently died and the executors were anxious to rid themselves of a bunch of expensive hungry animals. Armed with a list of the horses, I retired gratefully to my bed. It seemed another age since I had been in the dreamland world of mice, dogs and Popeye.

Next morning the priority seemed to be to equip myself with some clothing that would keep out at least some of the icy blast. Joining my friend for breakfast I mentioned this to him. He told me not to worry as the attorney's wife had realised my predicament and had promised to send some suitable clothing with her husband when he came to pick us up. She was as good as her word, and the attorney arrived with a coat that resembled a bear skin, and probably was just that. In addition he had found a rather moth eaten hat of the type worn by Russian politicians. Draping myself in the coat, I found that it had clearly been made for a very large bear. It reached down to my toes so that every step was a perilous move. Further, my hands were hidden in the voluminous sleeves.

In my new garb I shuffled out to the car and gratefully divested myself of the coat to relax in the centrally heated limousine. We drove for some thirty miles over iced ruts with two foot of snow on the surrounding fields until we arrived at the stud farm. The horses were all in their boxes in a large covered barn. As we got out of the car I resumed my bear-like look. Now, all vets have a routine for examining horses for a prospective purchaser. This begins by an in-hand trot to identify any lameness. This is again continued by a period of exercise to show any further breathing problems or other signs of lameness. With all this in mind I began to view the situation with some misgivings. My first dilemma became obvious in that I could not get my hands out of my coat far enough to hold a stethoscope or feel any of the legs of the horses. There was nothing for it but to withdraw from my friendly bear skin and risk the chance of frost bite. Having appraised the animals in their stables, I suggested that we have each horse out to trot it up. This was viewed with some dismay by the staff, since apart from a narrow passage in the bar, there was no possibility of taking any animal outside. Without doubt that would have speeded up the selection since at least a quarter of the number would have slipped and hurt themselves, being more than a little fresh after several days incarceration in their stables.

A Californian Caper

A compromise was agreed in that we would weed out those with obvious conformation defects. This resulted in a short list of some fifteen animals, which was further reduced by leaving two mares, which unfortunately were not in foal. Climbing back into my coat I found a brazier in the groom's room where I could bring some feeling back into my fingers. Whilst reviving my circulation the two protagonists agreed on a price for the thirteen horses, who were duly to be despatched home.

We then adjourned to our hotel to seal the deal with a handsome meal and a few drinks. I apologised to my friend for what had seemed to me to be a rather fruitless journey to the frozen north. Thankfully he was kind enough to say that my presence had enabled him to share the responsibility - a view with which I was not entirely happy. As the erstwhile horse dealer was anxious to return to his more usual role as an amateur rider in England on the next day, I set off once more to the airport to find a plane to San Francisco. I was due to rejoin my party at a hotel in Monterey, and then continue to explore the delights of the northern Sierra Nevada before beginning the serious object of our tour.

After spending a night in Vancouver I reached San Francisco, where I was to change planes for a local flight to Monterey. Walking through the airport I experienced another unexpected delight when I passed an elderly man struggling with a heavy suitcase. I offered to carry it for him to immigration, and he gratefully accepted. It was only as I handed him back the case that I recognised him to be none other than Bing Crosby.

Arriving at ten o'clock at Monterey I set off for the hotel at which the others were staying. To my surprise they had all retired to bed. I was to discover next morning that they had been down to New Mexico, where Montezuma had taken some of his revenge on the party. Feeling quite fresh after my journey I strolled down to the beach to find the most idyllic scene. The beach was a natural semicircle with the full moon shining over the smooth waters of the Pacific Ocean. If ever a sight cried out for some female companionship! Hollywood could not have devised a more romantic backcloth. However reality struck and I made my way back to the hotel with my dreams.

The next morning we all clambered aboard our bus and drove up into the mountains, where my companions looked with delight at the snow covered fields. My views were not so rose coloured and I was pleased that at least the temperature was not that of Calgary. Next morning we spent some time gazing in amazement at the giant size of the Sequoia trees, whose trunks were wide enough for at least fifteen men to surround with their arms.

Once more we embarked for our journey to Sacramento and Davis University. We travelled down from the mountains through fertile farmlands for an hour, when the bus without any warning came to a stop. No habitation was in sight, and the driver was at a loss to know what had upset his engine. We made various helpful comments such as whether he had run out of fuel, or whether the battery was flat, to which he turned a deaf ear merely saying that he would walk to the nearest telephone for help. Watching him depart we stepped off the bus to sit in the sun and await developments. After some minutes our silent lugubrious Scottish companion at last ventured to speak. Would we like a small dram to pass the time, as he had brought along a little of the Scottish yellow wine? Three of us agreed that this would certainly help to brighten the shining hour, and he went back to his seat, returning with four bottles of Glenlivet in a presentation case from the duty free in Heathrow. Remarking that he had managed to keep his possessions quiet for so long a time, we helped ourselves to a small dram.

By now the heat was getting stronger and our thirst was becoming all the greater. The original small dram was augmented by two or three slightly larger drams, but still there was no sign of our driver. The two students, who had up to now been impeccably behaved, spied three horses in a paddock behind us. Emboldened by the whisky they suggested we hold a horse race. Without further discussion, they and another single vet vaulted over the fence to catch the unsuspecting horses. To my surprise this was accomplished with more ease that I could ever manage when trying to catch my wife's ponies at home. The three intrepid, if foolhardy, jockeys all managed to climb on their selected horse and tried to set off up the paddock as though headed for the winning post down the Rowley Mile at Newmarket. One lasted no more than a few yards before his mount decided that it was too warm for racing. The other two continued up the field until one horse decided that the grass was greener at the bottom and whipped around dropping his unwanted pilot. The third horse on the contrary came to the conclusion that if this unsought rider really wished to race he would continue despite the jockey's unavailing attempts to stop him. He reached the far boundary where he whipped round and deposited his discomfited companion over the fence onto some rocks.

Whilst all this was in progress our driver returned to say that he had made contact with a garage who would be out in fifteen minutes. This good news warranted another round of Glenlivet. True to his work the garage mechanic arrived to see to the problem. Alas, he took one look at the name of the bus company and said that he was damned if he was going to help, since the company already owed him a sizable sum of money. Despite our pleas he was unbending and promptly drove off in a cloud of dust. It seemed that it was time we took matters into our own hands, and the tour director, claiming to have some knowledge of the entrails of a bus, climbed into the driver's seat. Turning on the engine he immediately noticed that the fuel gauge was reading a definite empty. The driver, facing the combined wrath of the whole party reluctantly agreed to walk back to the garage and collect a gallon of fuel. Once more we returned to the solace of the whisky bottle.

Eventually the bus was adequately refuelled for its journey to Sacramento. We had boarded again in various differing stages of health, one student rubbing his lower anatomy to ease the bruises which he suffered when decanted onto the rocks. Most of the party who had been imbibing the whisky retired to sleep it off. Unfortunately, and to my everlasting shame, I decided that the remainder of the group, who were disgruntled at the delay, needed cheering up. I made my way to the front of the bus and picking up the microphone proceeded to regale them with a variety of songs. These were sung in a voice that would not have won a place in the final of any talent competition. To my surprise and chagrin I could not persuade any of the party to join in. I assumed that they did not know the words, and thus their reluctance to show their ignorance. Little did I realise that they heartily wished I would shut up and go to sleep with my fellow addicts. To the relief of all we finally arrived at our hotel, and I made a rapid exit to my room. Awaking next morning with a monumental headache, I struggled down for several cups of black coffee. Unfortunately I decided to sit up at the counter. I was joined by a large and extremely healthy looking American, who proceeded to order a full American fried breakfast. The sight of a large steak was too much for my delicate stomach, and I made a speedy departure from the coffee room.

Arriving at the University to begin our further education, we were shown into the operating theatre where a major abdominal operation was in progress. The intestines were displayed on a washing tray, allowing the surgeon to remove a considerable length of incarcerated bowel. Not a good start for my delicate state. However I managed to overcome my queasiness sufficiently to ask some reasonable questions as to the quantities of intravenous fluid they were administering to the patient. This was something new to me, and I was pleased to be able to take a new technique back to our own hospital. As the day wore on, I began to feel a lot better, although I was not surprised that several members of the group treated me like a pariah.

The remainder of the day was spent in discussions of new methods of treatment. It was obvious that at that time we had a lot to learn from the other side of the water. Being a major equine hospital they had access to much sophisticated equipment that was way beyond our limited pockets. I met with a number of veterinarians there who in future years I would get to know, and with whom I would work more closely. As we left to go to our hotel for the conference I felt that it had been a day well spent and fully justified my absence from the practice at home, even if some of the previous jaunts would take some explaining to my partners. The four day conference was certainly worthwhile, although it consisted of numerous short papers with little time for any discussion. As usual you learned more from informal talks with your colleagues outside the lecture hall. The social side was adequately cared for and allowed us time to see the sights of that remarkable city. We were lucky enough to stay at the Top of the Mark, one of the best sited hotels in the world. The view from the revolving bar on the top floor was breathtaking.

One of the vets whom we met with was an elderly character endowed with a natural gift as a raconteur. He had led a varied life, starting as a cowboy on a ranch in Arizona. Eventually he gravitated to Hollywood where he acted as consultant vet for a film company. One of his tales illustrates many of his amusing experiences. He was looking after the horses for the film Ben Hur. The director wished to shoot the chariot race in Italy, and all the horses were flown out from America. Unfortunately one of the horses, a grey, was afflicted by a parasite, which lived by burrowing beneath the skin. This caused small areas of blood to be extruded from their burrows. When the filming started, the grey horse came out with several streaks of blood on its neck. The director shouted for the vet to "get that bleeding horse cleaned up". As fast as the vet swabbed off the offending splodges on its neck and returned it to the set, more spots appeared. This continued for some time until the director became infuriated and ordered the vet to fly the horse home and bring another undamaged animal to his set for the race. No wonder films are expensive to make.

After a few other experiences, such as being taken by our friend from the southern Californian desert for an evening in an Irish bar, and then being driven back in his car up to what seemed like the tenth floor of the hotel, where he parked the car in a most unusual car park, we made our return journey home without further incident. It was a cultural shock to get back to work, and more so to meet my wife again. Poor girl, she had spent the time surrounded by builders who were adding an extension onto our house. This had necessitated the outer wall being removed, leaving her to the mercy of the December wind and rain. No wonder she was not madly keen to learn of my doings abroad.

CHAPTER 7
Adventures in Australasia (1970's)

I became interested in Australia many years ago when my wife and I were hosts to an Australian veterinary surgeon and his wife. He was on a world tour to broaden and up-date his knowledge of equine veterinary science. Realising that he did not practise in one of the metropolitan areas of Australia, I believed that we in Lambourn could show him modern horse practice. On the second day my partners were about to operate on a fractured fore leg of a racehorse. This entailed the administration of a general anaesthetic to enable the limb to be repaired with a plate and screws.

Now it happened that we had just obtained a new gas anaesthetic machine. This was to be the third time it would be used, and we were still novices in the technique. The procedure involved the insertion of a tube through the horse's mouth and down its windpipe. The tube was then connected to the anaesthetic gas to achieve sufficient relaxation for the operation to begin. One of the quirks of this type of anaesthesia was that the horse would appear to cease breathing as soon as the gas was turned on. To us this was a cause of some alarm. Was it still alive? Frantic search for a heartbeat ensued, until the animal began to breath again.

While this drama was ensuing, my Australian friend, who was standing quietly in the corner of the operating area, nodded to me and asked why we had not installed a heart monitor to record the heart action during induction of anaesthesia. I professed ignorance of this, and he explained that he always used this machine at home. At this I suddenly felt very small and humble. I had thought we were supposed to be impressing him and not vice versa. I immediately appreciated that I was going to have to revise my impression of the Australian scene. The wild outback with its alleged rough and ready approach to life was obviously not typical, and I resolved then to widen my knowledge of this far distant continent.

My first chance came after I had left the practice, when I was invited to talk to the Thoroughbred Breeders of South Australia about the new disease in mares which had broken out in England. It seemed an ideal opportunity for my wife to accompany me on a busman's holiday. She had for many years been breeding Welsh Mountain ponies and, through her showing, had met a number of Australian breeders. On learning that we proposed to visit their country she was asked if she would like to judge at one of their larger breed shows. To my delight she agreed and was even prepared to put her life at risk in an aeroplane.

In order to emphasise my pleasure that she was coming, I decided for the one and only time in my life to launch out and obtain first class fares for the long flight across the world. We duly arrived at Heathrow to be ushered into the first class lounge. This was my first mistake. From then on Wendy expected similar treatment whenever we flew again. We boarded the plane and sat back to enjoy unaccustomed luxury. The plane was due to make its first stop in Bahrain. There we got off for the routine hour's stop for re-fuelling. To my surprise I noticed as I glanced out of the airport lounge window two Bahraini engineers climbing up into one of the massive jet engines. There they proceeded to remove pieces of the engine like a child would dismantle a Meccano toy.

I thought better of pointing this out to Wendy, as I had the feeling that it would not enhance her belief in the safety of air transport. After some minutes the tannoy announced that there would be some delay to the flight from England to Sydney due to a minor technical problem. Although this seemed a classic understatement, I assured my wife that all would be in order, and that I had found such occurrences not unusual on previous flights. In true airport fashion we waited for a further hour until again the tannoy informed us that the little problem was taking longer than had been hoped to rectify.

We would therefore be taken to a nearby hotel for supper and a bed until three o'clock next morning when we would resume our journey. Hooray for first class. At least we would not have to spend the next six hours in the terminal.

Next morning we were returned to the airport and re-boarded our plane. The captain apologised for the delay and said we would make up what time we could. Meanwhile we enjoyed an excellent breakfast and watched the coast of the Emirates disappear behind us. Half an hour later the captain again came on the intercom to tell us that we had suffered a further piece of bad luck. As opposed to the inner starboard engine of last night, we now seemed to have lost power in the outer starboard engine and would have to return to Bahrain. This we duly did, to be met by a screaming team of fire engines and ambulances careering down the runway. By now not only Wendy but also myself had begun to lose confidence in our choice of airlines. My own confidence had waned when the captain had come through to our compartment to reassure us, and I had realised that the last time I had seen him was when he had rammed his out-of-control yacht straight into the club commodore's boat, which had been moored off the pontoon by the yacht club on the Hamble river.

Fortunately the problem with this engine proved to be minor and we were shortly aboard and headed safely for our next stop in Singapore. We had already booked a hotel room for one night prior to catching the next flight on to Sydney the following evening. Our surprise was total when we were shown into the royal suite. Assured by the smiling porter that there was no mistake, we made up for the vicissitudes of the flight by deciding which of the three beds we would use and helping ourselves to a welcoming glass of champagne. Things would undoubtedly improve from now on. Little did we know what the morrow would bring.

On the short journey from the airport to the hotel, we had been warned by our driver that we should be careful not to leave anything unattended while in Singapore. Thus warned, Wendy decided that from many years experience I was not to be trusted with any important possessions. Forthwith she took command of the passports and all our money and travellers' cheques. For some unknown reason I agreed to this slur on my capabilities with no demur. The next morning we decided to take a bus tour to see a little of the island on our first visit. We duly toured the Tiger Balm gardens and the impressive sights of the place. Getting off the bus at the hotel, I arranged with a colleague of mine, who was senior vet at Bukit Timor racecourse, to continue my education in the afternoon. As I walked back to Wendy, she was ashen faced.

"I have left my bag with the passports on the bus. What can you do?"

My first thought was to go to the bar and demolish a large scotch. What were we to do in a strange place with no money and no passports?

Why is it that when abroad all the locals look alike? The hotel lobby was full of young men wearing white shirts and grey flannels. One of these approached me having realised that I was in some trouble. Asking if he could help, I explained our predicament. He told me not to worry and he would search for the bus. I immediately felt better, but not for long. The receptionist in whom I had also confided, said I was mad to give a stranger all that information. I would certainly not see the bag again. Devastated, I made again for the bar to replenish my glass. If I was to be imprisoned or deported at least I could go intoxicated. I then rang my friend to cancel his kind invitation to the racecourse and began to wonder whether the British consul would be in any way sympathetic. We spent the afternoon in a complete daze, in my case helped by more whisky, in Wendy's by counting her remaining minutes of freedom. At five o'clock the receptionist called me to the desk. He had received a call from the bus office to say that my wife's bag was in their hands and would I collect it. Never before nor since have I made such speed to an assignation. Wonderful to relate there was the bag and all the contents were intact. From then on I took charge of these and strange to say, Wendy did not in the least object.

Feeling at least ten years older, we returned to the airport and gratefully fell into our seats for the final stage of the journey. We arrived over Sydney harbour in the early morning and all my dreams came true. The sun was shining and there was the famous bridge and the Opera House. I knew even then that this was not to be my last visit. I was sure that one of my goals in life would one day be achieved. This particular goal was to sail a yacht under the Sydney bridge, and I am pleased to say that a few years later I was able to do that very thing, toasting the bridge in a cold tin of Toohey's beer. We were met by a charming lady from the show at which Wendy was going to judge in two days time. She took us to a comfortable motel in a suburb called Maroubra. There we did totally the wrong thing and decided to catch up on some sleep. Little did I know then that the only way to conquer jet lag is to fight on through the day and collapse in bed at the same time as the locals do. As a result we slept most of the day and spent the first night awake. Much as I now love Australia, I must say that their television is even more trying than that in America. At least by the end of the night we knew everything that could be bought at supermarkets and had endless opportunities to memorise the various brands of washing powder.

Wendy had a few pony breeder contacts whom she had met at home and I knew about four veterinary surgeons in the bloodstock world. One of those was a man who had worked for me for a few months some years before. I telephoned him at the practice in Sydney and suggested we meet, and could he pick me up. He enquired where we were staying and I told him the address. His response was not encouraging.

"Maroubra. Where the hell is Maroubra?"

When I told him that it was the next bay along from Bondi, he thought he could find us. When he came to pick me up and took me back to the practice I noted that it was a ten minute ride. I had thought the Australians counted distances in hours of driving. Obviously they did not reckon on short distances being within their compass. I spent the day with Trevor and was interested to note that the problems with their racehorses almost exactly mimicked those of ours at home. The next day we were invited to visit Randwick racecourse. I was introduced to one of the leading trainers as an English vet. His reply was that they did not need any more vets, but what they needed were plumbers. Could I not change my occupation?

On the following morning Wendy's work began in earnest. The classes were full of lovely ponies, which would certainly not have been out of place at the Royal Welsh Show. Indeed a number of them had been imported from the UK. I spent the day taking cine films of the various classes. A pointless occupation as it turned out, since the camera was later lost in Sydney and the films defeated my attempts to change them, resulting in most of them being spoilt by the sunlight. Cinematography has never been one of my strong points. As a result of the show we were invited to visit a number of studs and spent many happy days being royally entertained by differing generous hosts. We made a great number of new friends with whom we were to revisit on several occasions in years to come.

One of my initial disappointments was that of not meeting any native Australians who spoke the 'Strine' we had heard about at home in the music hall vogue. On our return to Sydney I telephoned a veterinary friend of mine who had seen practice with us at Lambourn as a student. He was now senior partner in a large thoroughbred breeding area some two hundred miles north of Sydney. It was a surprise to me that he had even entered horse practice. I remembered his introduction to equine practice with me when I took him to castrate some ten Welsh ponies for a local farrier. These were housed for our convenience in a small chicken shed. I suggested that he and Healey should go in and catch them while I got the equipment ready. After a few minutes they both emerged covered from head to toe in chicken feathers with none of the ponies captured.

"If that is horse practice," he stuttered, blowing feathers from his lips, "you can keep it. I will concentrate on clean small animal hospitals."

Having then helped to throw ropes over the creatures as they spun around the walls of the shed, we managed to complete our task, but my assistant was still not impressed and continued to mutter on the way home that we could keep our work as it was not for him. Obviously the atmosphere in Australia had altered his attitude.

However to return to my story, when I rang the practice I was answered by a thick Australian voice. On introducing myself and explaining that I would like to come and visit them, he said,

"Oh, too right, my oath! Come as soon as you like. We can arrange to have you both stay up here."

I said we would be with them in a couple of days.

"Fair dinkum, that'll be right," he answered. This was a delight to me to hear the genuine colloquial talk. The only odd point was that I knew that my correspondent was a Scottish graduate who had only been in the country for a year.

Wendy and I set off for the area renowned for its horses and even more for its wine. Both more than lived up to our expectations. I had spent many years at home on breeding farms, where the breeding season for horses began in February and continued relentlessly to July, so it was with considerable envy that I found my colleagues working in temperatures up in the low eighties. Not for them the freezing mornings spent in one's shirt sleeves waiting until another recalcitrant mare was coaxed into the examination box. This was breeding practice made easy. No stables requiring endless labour to clean them out each day. Instead mares and foals ran out in large paddocks only being brought into wooden stock yards for an assessment as to whether they were ready for presentation to the stallion. They were encouraged to walk down a race next to a 'teaser' colt, whose unfortunate role in life was merely to select the wives for his more illustrious male companions. By six o'clock in the morning the day's list for mating was concluded. At home this operation was much more labour intensive, requiring each mare to be caught and led into a barn to be introduced to the teaser. The whole procedure was unlikely to be finished by ten o'clock.

Another welcome beauty of the system was that all the mares were allowed to foal naturally out in a paddock close to the stud groom's house. Lights were fixed around the perimeter of the paddock so no close supervision was necessary unless a problem was noted. The foals would be born into temperatures more conducive to good health than those met by foals at home, who were just as likely to meet snow and icy winds on their first visit to the outside world.

True the system was not without some problems, which we did not meet at home. Due to the dry and sometimes dusty environment the foals were liable to infection with a bacterium causing abscesses to develop in their lungs. However the pluses well outweighed the minuses and I was sold on the idea of breeding horses in such a climate. In years to come it would be fashionable and eminently economic to fly top quality stallions out for the breeding season in the southern hemisphere, where they covered mares from September to just after Christmas, allowing them to return to Europe in time to recommence their work in February. This system of so-called 'shuttle stallions' had just begun at the time of my first visit to the continent, and one of the theories current at home was that the new breeding disease was occasioned by the stallions having picked up this infection in Australia and carried it back to us. When I arrived in Adelaide to talk to the breeders there about our problems, I was rapidly disabused of such ideas. They had documentation to prove that their problem stemmed without any doubt to two imported stallions from home. Reluctantly in the face of their evidence I could only agree that we must have been at fault. Despite all this I was welcomed and shown around a number of delightful studs.

The great asset of the small equine community was that however far from home, one met contacts who were to remain good friends for many years. As an example of what a small world it has become - many years later on a further visit, I called at a large stud to have a look at what I knew to be one of the leading establishments in the world, let alone just in Australia. I was told beforehand to ask for a girl called June, who was assistant to the manager and would show us around. On meeting her, she asked where we lived in England. When I mentioned that we lived close to a village called Lambourn, she asked if I knew a cousin of hers who lived in the village. To my surprise not only did I know him, but he was one of my closest friends to whose daughter I was godfather. Equally coincidental was that when we returned to the office, standing there was another acquaintance of mine, now working for a bloodstock agency. Not only had he bred Welsh ponies but I had sold him a thoroughbred brood mare who went on to breed a classic winner in Hungary for him.

Being sold on the climate, the hospitality of the people, and the relaxing way of like, it was not surprising that I was to pay many more visits to such an attractive continent. Indeed I have now notched up some eight journeys to Australia. Not all have been blessed with unqualified success. I have still to see the Barrier Reef in all its glory. We mistakenly planned one year to spend an exotic Christmas in Cairns with my daughter and her husband. This unhappily coincided with the arrival of cyclone Joy on the north eastern coast. Wendy and I spent three worrying days in Darwin knowing that our daughter was ensconced in Cairns, then besieged by one hundred and fifty kilometre winds. Fortunately we all eventually met up in Townsville on Christmas Day in rain such as I had never before experienced. We made our escape in a hired car through various towns to Brisbane; each town being declared a disaster zone on our departure. The remainder of the holiday seemed to be spent in the car driving some three thousand miles. One can easily forget just how large the country is. Age and common sense has now taught me to limit my journeying to more manageable proportions.

Some five years after my first visit to the continent I managed to persuade the authorities in Switzerland that I was just the person to be appointed as Foreign Veterinary Surgeon to the first international Three Day Event to be held in Australia. The position as Foreign Vet involved seeing that firstly the rules of the International Equestrian Federation were obeyed during the competition and also to ensure that the welfare of the horses was safeguarded throughout. The further considerable complication with this Event, was that the Australians had never faced the possibility of some fifty or sixty horses descending on them from varying parts of the outside world. Quite naturally the authorities there were very cautious about allowing horses into the country with the ever present risk of bringing new diseases in with them. Australasia for instance is the only continent in the world where equine influenza is not endemic.

In order to see to the necessary arrangements I was asked to accompany one of the judges for the Event on a visit to South Australia at the time of their own annual Event one year prior to the International. My first task was to liaise with the quarantine authorities, who insisted on all the foreign horses being quarantined for two weeks on their arrival. Since it would be vital that some facilities could be made available for exercise and training before the actual competition, we had to try and alter the existing layout of the quarantine stations. In order to accommodate all the horses it was decided to fly half into Sydney and the remainder into South Australia. I was delighted to find the local authorities had entered into this with the enthusiasm and co-operation which I would not have expected from those at home. They set about laying down gallops and ordering show jumps with such gusto that I had to point out to them that these horses would have flown twelve thousand miles without a stop, and for the first week at least would require no more than gentle walking and trotting exercise. However, I agreed that a suitable area for cantering on the second week would be advantageous, although I thought it unlikely that show jumping would be on their agenda at that time.

The willingness of the vets at the quarantine stations led me to believe that we should be able to achieve at least good health if not complete fitness for the incoming mounts. Except for a very limited number of racehorses, nobody had attempted such distances for equine athletes before, and it was very much an unknown field as to what effect air travel would have on such highly tuned animals. In fact the whole operation was entirely successful and laid down a template for future long distance travel for a variety of competing horses. It is, as we now know, commonplace for racehorses to travel out for races such as the prestigious Melbourne Cup. This exercise was to prove valuable experience for me when I had to make similar arrangements for the Olympic Games in Korea, of which more will be told.

Once having settled the quarantine facilities I joined my fellow travellers to view the Event, which was due to start in two days time. On the competition site the stables, the security, and the cross country course were my areas of concern. The stabling to be provided was no problem;

however the security of the horses at the actual Event site was in considerable need of improvement. As originally laid out it allowed any spectator to wander through the compound. With the strict enforcement of doping regulations it was imperative that only those immediately connected with the horses should be allowed access to the area.

The cross country course was not yet built for the big competition, but a review of the proposed area led to worries that the ground might be far too hard for the horses. Various suggestions were made for the improvement of especially the take-off and landing areas around the obstacles. Throughout our preliminary investigations the local officials were helpful, if a little querulous as to why we were being (to them) so pedantic. I learned a little of the Australian temperament at that time, which I am sure my many Australian friends will not mind me restating. At first they exuded confidence at their ability to put on a first class competition. They could not understand our worries about security, or even those of our press colleagues, who insisted on greater facilities being arranged for them. As the days continued, their confidence seemed to lapse, and on the third day, one of the officials, a large amiable sheep farmer, came up to me and asked confidentially did I believe that they could manage to put on a show comparable with Badminton Horse Trials.

"You must remember that we people out here are eight hours from bugger all."

I assured him that all would be well on the night, but I did not believe that they would get similar crowds to the quarter of a million at Badminton. Unfortunately they did cater for far too many people the next year, resulting in a deal of unnecessary expense.

As we sat down to watch the dressage phase, I asked the American judge who was with me to give me an idea of his scoring of the various competitors. This he did, only to be rendered speechless when two of the competitors jumped over the small fence at the boundary of the dressage ring to disappear over the horizon. An Australian on my other side laughed and explained that the local horseman did not go much on dressage. They certainly have improved in the intervening years, collecting gold medals at two Olympics.

We finally left the site with a feeling of optimism for the next year's Event, which was to be borne out in full. On our return a year later I was relieved to see the horses emerge from quarantine in superb health. The riders and grooms had nothing but praise for the quarantine officers and their facilities. As soon as I reached the competition site I was asked by one of the organisers if I could go and talk with the RSPCA official since one of the Animal Rights Group had announced their intention of sitting down in front of the fences to disrupt the proceedings. I was unsure if my presence would make any difference to this threat, but yet again I had underestimated the smallness of the equine world. I walked forward to where the inspector was standing and started to introduce myself.

"Oh there is no need for that," he laughed, "I remember you all right, Dr Frank. I worked as travelling head lad at Manton Stables near Marlborough for many years before coming out here. Now that I know that you are in charge I will tell the protestors that there is no need for them to cause any disruption."

Realising that I did recognise his face, even if I could not have placed him, I was far less confident in his assertion that my presence would avert any disasters. Fortunately his prediction was to come true and the three days went off without more than some small hitches.

One minor drama took place out of earshot of the public, when I had given over my courtesy Mitsubishi cross country car to the organiser, Mr Tricket, who wished to convey the State Governor in some degree of comfort around the course. As I listened to the intercom in a colleague's car we heard a plaintive call on one of the lavatory attendants' portable phone to his mate at another convenience station.

"Hello, dunny [Australian for portaloo] one calling dunny two. Are you receiving me?"

Back came the answer from his chum,

"Yes, dunny two here, receiving you loud and clear."

"Dunny two, has anybody been to empty your dunny yet? Mine is full with a long queue waiting to come in."

"Dunny two here. No, mine is the same, and we were told that we were to report to Mr Tricket for action."

They then decided that they must find the boss to get some relief. We fell off our seats laughing at the predicament of Tricket trying to organise this in the august presence of the Governor. Perhaps he would have been better advised to keep his own car without the ever present wireless communication.

The competition over without major worries on my part, Wendy and I took our leave and began a two weeks foray to our Australian friends. Once again I decided that a soujourn 'down under' was a welcome tonic from life in England.

Twenty years later on a further visit to Australia I attempted my last and definitely concluding venture into field surgery. Wendy and I were staying with a very great family friend who was a leading breeder of ponies and cattle. He had to our great delight, married a young, newly qualified veterinary surgeon some eighteen months before. To keep her hand in, she was working part time for the local practice. The night we arrived she was busy reading up the veterinary literature on operating on equine abdominal rigs. This entailed investigating the stomach cavity to search for an undescended testicle. Looking up from her reading she asked if I had ever done such operations. Like a complete idiot I said that I had performed quite a few when in practice. Indeed I had acquired such a reputation in the practice for locating obscure retained testicles in the abdomen that our yard man, Johnny Healey, had re-christened me "bollocky Bill".

On learning of my so-called expertise I was ordered to be up and ready to leave at seven o'clock the next morning. I woke in a cold sweat at the thought of what I had let myself in for. It was twenty years since I had last ventured my hand into the stomach of any horse. We drove to the farm and once again found a large reception committee. To my relief the owner greeted us by saying that if we could not find the missing object he would have the horse destroyed. This at least gave me some glimmer of confidence, since he clearly did not value his animal too highly.

The anaesthetic was administered by my colleague, aided by a very efficient lady nurse, who insisted on monitoring the heart beat throughout the operation. The horse was shaved and scrubbed over the site where I had tentatively pointed to for the incision. It transpired that my lady colleague's boss had removed one testicle some three years previously. After considerable questioning it was unanimously decided by all and sundry that he had removed the right testicle so that our quarry was lying hidden some where on the left. The incision was made, and the chief surgeon got up and suggested that I use my expertise in tracing the missing organ. I plunged my hand into the hidden depths and felt the usual mass of intestines and other impedimenta which lie in the cavity. In vain did I search for anything which resembled my prey. At that stage another young vet came in arrayed, I was pleased to note, with long arms. I told him to try his luck as I could just feel a possible target with my finger tips away down on the right hand side of the abdomen.

He duly took over from me and gave a shout of antipodean glee to indicate that he had his hand around what he thought could be the missing testicle. At that he changed places with me and indeed there was that for which we had been searching. It had always been my usual technique to insert a chain around the neck of the testicle and remove it by slowly tightening the chain. In this case I was offered instead a pair of crushing implements, which were more of use with a small sized dog or cat. With great difficulty and a lot of moaning about the shortcomings of far distance practices I eventually succeeded in removing the offending article and placing it on a sheet for the local photographer to snap it for posterity.

The operation was concluded with no further trouble, and the now complete gelding rose to his feet within a short time, apparently none the worse for his ordeal. Only at that time did the owner express his delight and vouchsafe that he had in fact sold the horse for five thousand dollars should we be successful. I congratulated the assembled crowd, remarking that it was a pity that peoples' memory was so vague that they could not recall right from left.

For somebody with no claims to surgery, it seemed that now was definitely the time to call a halt while I was still just ahead. Wendy and I intend to visit the continent one more time, for we still have to see the Barrier Reef in all its glory and a visit to the Melbourne Cup is another goal yet to be achieved.

CHAPTER 8
Assignation to Arabia (1970's)

After leaving the practice as a full time partner I agreed to look after the veterinary side of several stud farms. One of these was owned by a well-known entrepreneur who had considerable business dealings in the oil world in the Middle East. The idea was mooted that he should start up an agricultural company to develop crop growing in Saudi Arabia. To this end he enlisted the help of the farm manager on the stud, and suggested that I might like to become involved as an advisor to any livestock enterprise which might materialise.

Since I had never been to that part of the world it sounded an interesting challenge. In order to examine the situation I was invited to join the boss on a tour of Kuwait and Saudi Arabia. Included in the party was the stud manager, Dave Dick, who had long been a friend of mine. In my early days in Lambourn he had been a leading National Hunt jockey, and as such was held in some awe by me, since I had enormous admiration for anybody brave enough to daily risk their necks in that most hazardous of callings. As I got to know him better, I discovered that he had a unique personality. Equally at home at a jellied eel stall in the East End of London as he was dining at the Ritz or the Berkeley, he not only had a great knowledge of horses but a splendid capacity and zest for life in general. In his company I was sure that the projected visit would be entertaining even if not to prove fruitful for our intended purpose.

I met the rest of the party in the first class lounge at Heathrow, which seemed an auspicious beginning to what was to be an unusual journey. We boarded the plane and sat in extreme comfort to Kuwait City. Emerging from the plane we were ushered into a large black Cadillac at the foot of the stairway and driven to the VIP lounge. Our passports were collected and we were led to the welcoming party, which was headed by a sheikh, one of the ruler's brothers. A man in his late thirties, speaking perfect English, he was in time to become a great friend. The Sheikh was a perfect foil for my ex-jockey companion, with the same twinkle in his eye as he welcomed us to his country. As we got to know him better we learned that he was an avid sportsman and moreover a keen racing enthusiast, training some forty Arab racehorses just outside the city limits. He was president of the national soccer team, which at that time was not far short of world class. In the next two years the team was to reach the later rounds of the next World Cup, urged on from the touchline by Sheikh Fahad.

Our leader owned an apartment in the City, where he had a business running, and to there we went for our stay of three days in the most modern of Middle Eastern cities. I discovered that this visit was in the nature of a rest-break before the serious objective in Saudi Arabia. As such we were treated very much in the habit to which I could easily become accustomed, sitting in the best seats at the football stadium, spending a day's fishing on the royal yacht in the Persian Gulf and enjoying some typical Arabian picnics in the splendid black tents, which were a common sight in that part of the world. The etiquette of an Arab meal took some getting used to. Eating with the right hand, and sitting for several hours with one's knees curled up lest one presented the forbidden sight of the soles of the feet to those sitting opposite. The old story of the chief guest being presented with a sheep's eye proved entirely mythical, at least in this company.

Following the dinner Sheikh Fahad took us around his horses, which were stabled on two sides of the area where the tent had been set up. Suddenly I was to be asked to use my expertise in diagnosis. He showed us a three year old colt, with which he hoped to win the big race on the next day at the local racecourse. The head man, a lovable old Pakistani, said he had not eaten up all his night feed. Hoping that our party had put him off his feed, I went in to examine him. His temperature was raised and his eye membranes were a distinct yellow. Realising that this was a case of jaundice I warned the owner that he was most unlikely to race the next day. On being asked what they should do for the horse, I said that unless we could take a blood test I could not be sure what was wrong with him. Thinking that this would give me some time to work out the cause of the jaundice, I said that perhaps tomorrow we could investigate the trouble. Alas, I had reckoned without the power of the ruling classes in this little kingdom. Fahad immediately told me to get some blood and we would take it to the medical laboratory in town. With that we set off in the stable run-about, a blue Rolls Royce, no more than two years old, a car that I was to get to know well in months to come as I drove it recklessly across the desert. By the time we had reached the laboratory I had recalled that tick borne diseases might be prevalent in this part of the world. Caused by small protozoa which invaded the red blood cells, the disease resembled malaria and would require a special injection to remove the infecting organism. Sure enough the blood sample revealed the tell-tale protozoa in the sample. I agreed that I would try and get some of this drug on my return to England. This was in no way quick enough for the Sheikh, so next morning I got on the phone to home to arrange for some to be despatched to Kuwait by air. Not so easy unfortunately. The drug was not available in England, so I rang the manufacturers, who said they could get some sent on from India where there was a supply.

This was my first encounter with what was possible when a powerful man wished something to be done in a hurry. A more amusing episode occurred some months later when I met Fahad in his suite at a London hotel. His football team were preparing for the World Cup and he wanted a top English team to come out the next week to play a friendly match against them. Would I please arrange this? Now, I knew little about soccer and certainly did not seem to be in the position to get that which he required. However, I did know one of the directors of Chelsea Football Club. Ringing him with this strange request he thought it could well be arranged. With a weight off my mind I joyfully reported that indeed Chelsea would come out to play. The immediate answer took my breath away.

"I don't want a second rate team, I want Manchester United, Liverpool or Arsenal!"

Reluctantly I picked up the phone and rang the Arsenal office. I was put through to the secretary and explained my rather ludicrous request. Apologising for troubling him I said I would of course understand if he declined, as I realised that he was in the middle of their very busy season. To my complete amazement he thought it would be possible for them to fly out on Monday, play on Tuesday and fly back the next day. There was only one problem, due to insurance policies, the whole team could not fly on the same plane. I assured him that since I believed that the Sheikh owned Kuwait Air, they could probably have a plane each. I reported back to the eager team manager, who then asked that I phone again to ensure that only the full first team would come and not a second eleven. At this I decided to bow out and leave him to meet the secretary and arrange what he wanted. Amazingly the whole episode worked and what was even better, Kuwait won the match by one goal. I now appreciate that one should never take no for a final answer.

The next morning I returned to the stables and gave the horse some antibiotics and vitamin injections to tide him over until the new drug arrived. Thankfully he seemed no worse than the night before. We then got into the Rolls and were taken across the desert to Fahad's stud farm. This in reality was a euphemism since all it consisted of was a range of boxes and some sand paddocks railed off with scratch wooden fences. The mares numbered around twenty and were all in good health. The person in charge was a personal friend of the owner's who knew the mares well, but had no training in the management of a stud farm. The main problem was that he had no idea as to which, if any, of the mares were pregnant. Could I please examine them and let them know how things stood. I explained that I had no gear for the job with me and anyway it would take some time to go through all the mares. At this they suggested that I return next week to carry out the examinations and to give further advice on the feeding of the young stock and racehorses. Thus began an intimate involvement with Sheikh Fahad, which lasted for the next three or four years.

Our party returned to the airport for our journey on to Saudi Arabia. I have been sufficiently ungallant previously in not mentioning that our group was made up by the wives of the boss and the stud manager. So the five of us were taken to the leader's private plane, which he had arranged to be in Kuwait for the trip to Riyadh. The flight was excellent until we were cleared for landing at the airport, when suddenly the pilot grabbed the controls to rapidly climb again. Looking out of the window, I saw to my horror a large jumbo taking off from the runway at which we had been aiming. It did not seem that air traffic control was all that it might be. From what I was going to see in Riyadh this was not at all surprising.

Once again we were greeted at the terminal as most important people. Ushered into the VIP suite, our chief host was the assistant Minister of Agriculture, under whose auspices we were to be working. Alongside him was an imposing man in his gold fringed disha dasha. He was a civil engineer by training and would act as our middle man and negotiator for any contract we might arrange. After a ceremonial welcome with special cups of very sweet tea which prefaced any discussion, we were driven through the city to a compound in the outskirts.

The car journey was fascinating. We began down a modern three lane highway, past a modern hotel. After less than a mile we moved onto dust roads winding through rows of romantic looking mud houses, such as one might see as a back drop for a production of The Desert Song. Passing a circular tower block of maybe ten stories, the engineer proudly told us that this new building housed his offices. Only then did I realise that what we had seen so far comprised virtually all the new construction sites in Riyadh. In fact the city had just six months before been opened to foreigners. Prior to then, it was only permissible for those of the Muslim faith to enter. The British Embassy had just been moved from Jeddah to Riyadh two months before our visit.

The road along which we drove was crowded with passers-by, still oblivious to the dangers of motor traffic - a situation that was rapidly to change as fleets of second-hand American cars became available to those who could afford them. I soon was to recognise that driving tests were at that stage not obligatory in the country. I viewed more accidents in three days there than one would see in a year at home. This culminated in a fifty kilometre drive the next day out to a farm, when we passed sixteen smashes, only to become the seventeenth victim ourselves in a ministry car which was ordered by the police to cross a line of traffic. Unfortunately, the policeman had failed to communicate to the other driver that it would be as well for him to stop to let us cross.

The compound where we were to stay was owned by a large gregarious man, who had made his fortune in hiring equipment for oil drilling. He welcomed us with open arms, having previously had dealings with our party leader. His English was basic, but just more than my Arabic which by then stretched no further than *"Salaam Alaikham"*. I was soon to have my vocabulary improved even if only by the dreaded word *"bukra"*, which I learned was the Arabic for *"mañana"*, and usually implied that whatever you requested might be granted sometime but not necessarily ever.

The next morning we were taken out to what purported to be the National Stud and experimental dairy farm. Situated fifteen kilometres out of the city centre, the complex was lying on flat land beneath a picturesque escarpment of red sandstone. It looked for all the world like the setting for a Hollywood western, and it was soon to be known to us as John Wayne country. On the other side of the road stood an imposing radio disk such as the one at Jodrell Bank at home. We were impressed to note such modern technology. The denouement came some time later when we realised that the position of the reflector never altered. On questioning it was admitted that in truth the disk was not working since there was no electricity connected. This epitomised the situation in the capital at that time. Sad to say, the West had used the rapid increase in demand for all electrical goods as an excuse for a massive dumping ground for outdated equipment from washing machines to generators and agricultural equipment.

Our guide at the stud was the Palestinian assistant at the Agriculture Ministry, whose knowledge of horses was nil, in fact we believed that his knowledge of matters agricultural was little more. He picked his way delicately across the dirt paddock, holding his disha dasha tastefully around his knees. The stock consisted of around one hundred mares and five stallions. The latter were led out proudly for our inspection, and an impressive sight they made. Looking fat and well, they stood at a height more usual for English hunters than the Arabians to which we were accustomed.

On turning to the mares, Dave promptly burst into tears. One of his most endearing traits has always been an open show of all his emotions, whether pleased or horrified. I had to agree that the latter emotion was uppermost in my mind as I saw this collection of emaciated, weak animals. One push on their flank and they would all but fall over. To make the tragedy worse, the animals were fundamentally of good conformation and of a type that would do justice to any horse-loving home in England. We all agreed that this was a situation that we must attempt to deal with. The remainder of the farm consisted of some three hundred acres of sand, partitioned off into paddocks. The farm stock was a herd of Jersey cows in good condition but clearly not of prize stock.

The drive back to town found me wondering what could be done to improve the plight of the unfortunate mares. How were we to persuade the authorities to allow us to intervene? Fortunately the opportunity arrived on the following day by a strange set of circumstances. We were all invited to a special day at the city racecourse. Unlike the track in Kuwait, the stands were built of marble, and the track was overlaid with a generous helping of black oil, which greatly improved the going and made it such that the horses did not finish a mile race as though they had galloped for ten miles over deep plough. We were directed to comfortable armchairs behind the royal party. All went well until the third race, in which two horses finished upsides each other. Not to worry, we were told that the new photo finish camera would sort out which had won. We duly awaited for the arrival of the print being sent down from the camera team to the senior steward. Minutes went by, but still no action. After five more minutes a shamefaced man came running to the official's chair to report that he was sorry but they had forgotten to put the film in the camera. He seemed a nice man and very apologetic, so we trusted that he would awake next morning still in possession of both his hands.

The fourth race was the main event, and one of the royal party owned the well-fancied favourite. This was a big chestnut stallion, who was well-placed until the final furlong when he suddenly dropped out of the race, only to pull up lame on his left fore leg. We thanked our hosts for the afternoon and made our way back to change for the evening as we had all been invited to a party at one of the Ministry official's houses.

We had been advised to dress fairly smartly, which did not present me with a problem since I had only brought one suit with me, but the ladies were in some confusion as to what they should wear. The custom of the land decreed that no lady should show more than an ankle in the presence of company. Discreet western clothing was selected and we set off for the party. We arrived to find about fifteen couples present; the men in usual arabic dress, but the ladies in very smart Paris fashions. After a few minutes the telephone rang and an elderly man was summoned to speak. The call was from America, and the recipient turned to his friends with a request for the name of the best hotel in Seattle. To my surprise at least four of the company pulled out their diaries from under their cloaks and offered addresses and telephone numbers of favoured hotels in that distant city. The admixture of the old civilisation with such up-to-date knowledge of the western world was an indication of the speed with which that part of the globe was catching up with foreign events and customs.

We sat down to eat with accustomed cutlery and fine French cooking when the phone rang again. This time it was someone from one of the royal palaces. He understood that there was an English vet at the party, and his employer would like to see him straight away. Needless to say this was not a request that could be even momentarily ignored, so in the company of the boss and my companion, Dave, we set off for the palace. I was not sure whether the other two were coming for interest or to safeguard my health. At any rate I certainly valued their company since I had no idea what awaited me.

Arriving at the palace, we were directed towards a large tent in the grounds. Entering, we saw a number of armchairs arranged in a row on a sumptuous Persian carpet. To our amazement the walls and roof of the tent were covered in carpets of similar design, the whole being lit by a number of candelabra each holding long white wax candles. Seated in one of the chairs was the Sheikh, a tall impressive man with a hook nose, piercing eyes and a short manicured beard. I had noticed him at the races and presumed he was the owner of the horse which had pulled up lame. He waved us to the chairs and mint tea was promptly offered, this time in gold leaf cups. Our guide of yesterday introduced us in Arabic and apologised that the Sheikh could speak no English. He said that I should go and see the horse to advise the Sheikh as to what could be done for the injury which he had sustained in the race.

I said that of course I would be delighted to do this, so accompanied by my minders we followed another minion out of the tent and across a courtyard, lit in a gloom by burning tapers on stands. At the far end of the yard there sat four men, each beside a hooded falcon on its perch. The scene began to resemble a picture from a fairy tale of the Arabian Nights. We followed on through various other courtyards until we came on the stables. These were laid out in two rows of large loose boxes, very similar to those in an English racing stable, but all under cover and in an integral part of the palace.

As we walked through the passageway a short rotund man approached us and we were introduced to the trainer. He welcomed us and took us to the box where the chestnut horse was standing eating alfalfa. He was resting his left fore leg, which was encased in a thick bandage. A lad was summoned to take this off and I went forward to feel the damage. The tendons down the back of the leg were thickened from the knee to the fetlock with considerable heat and pain in the back tendon. I looked up and questioned the trainer as to whether this was a new injury or the recurrence of an old sprain. He laughed and told me through our interpreter that it had begun two years ago, and today's race was the first for twelve months. I shook my head and said that the prospects of a recovery to race again were at best remote. This seemed to accord with the trainer's views, so I said I would report back to the Sheikh. On the return to the palatial tent our businessman leader, ever with an eye to the main chance said that I should offer to operate on the leg. I firmly declined this offer since although the operation presented no problem, I was worried about the after care with the ever present chance of infection getting into the wound site. What the standard of veterinary care in Saudi was I did not know, but I suspected the risk of the horse suffering an infection and the end result being worse than the present injury, which would in any case not preclude the horse's use for stud.

Once more in the tent I explained through the interpreter what I had found. My pessimistic prognosis did not seem to take the Sheikh by surprise, and I continued to suggest what treatment I thought should be done to ease the present inflammation. On hearing my report, the Sheikh asked why it was that racehorses should suffer such injuries to their tendons, since he had ridden since a child at high speeds over the desert with its rocks and dunes without these problems. I tried to point out that the speed of a racehorse would in no way compare with that of a riding horse, and that the strains on the legs were that much greater. He then countered my argument that perhaps it was because racehorses wore shoes whereas his ridden Arabs were always unshod. This then involved us in an intricate discussion on the question of frog pressures as a means of dissipating the stresses on the legs. All this was far too much for our interpreter, and the Sheikh waved him aside indicating that he could perfectly understand what I was saying. Not bad for someone who spoke no English. Not only did he know his anatomy of the horse's foot, but he was clearly a very knowledgeable horseman.

It was at this point that I decided to bring the state of the horses at the National Stud into the conversation. Explaining their dire condition, my companions joined in to suggest that maybe we could help to improve the stud and make it more of a national asset and show place. It was obvious that the Sheikh had not seen the stud for a long time, and he was plainly horrified at our report. After considerably haranguing the wretched Ministry man it was decided that if we could get a team out to Riyadh next week we should have a free hand to develop the stud and farm. This we agreed to do without at that time having any idea how we could set about it.

As we got up to take our leave, I commented on the type of the mares at the stud, saying that they were not at all typical of the Arab horses that we saw at home. The Sheikh grinned and said that we should come and visit his own stud the next evening and he would show us his band of genuine Arabian horses which he had caught, running wild in the desert. Thanking him for this singular honour, we returned to the party well satisfied with the evening's outcome.

Leaving the businessman to conduct the discussions over contracts for the management of the stud, Dave and I went back to review what we should require to bring out from England, always supposing that we could muster a team of at least five good and true young lads to work out there. The first thing that we discovered was that there was virtually no feed for the hundred or so horses. It soon became apparent that the man in charge of the complex was responsible for collecting the money from the Finance Ministry. This money was to be used to pay the staff and the foodstuff and all other running expenses. It did not take us long to discover that rather than spend the money on the project, the manager was using it to make monthly visits to Lebanon, where he lived in some splendour on the proceeds.

Reporting this back to the engineer, who was now our contact man, he straight away arranged for the errant gentleman to be dismissed and for us to be authorised to collect the cash when we returned with our team. Apart from this major decision, we would have to organise some living accommodation for the team, and I would have to purchase the necessary medicaments essential for the improvement of the health of the animals.

The following afternoon, our last before heading back home, we assembled for our trip to the Sheikh's stud farm. We were told by several people what an honour this was, since the stud was never visited by anyone other than his own family. We arrived about one hour before sunset, and were taken around the stables by the man in charge. The 'genuine Arabians' of which we had been told the previous evening, were an impressive bunch of some twenty mares and young stock. Not as big as those on the National Stud, they were stocky with heads more of a dish-shaped type which we associated with European Arabs. How long they had been on the stud was not clear, but they formed a docile herd, surprising for animals which had been running loose about the desert.

We had just completed our tour when we were asked to return to the entrance where the Sheikh had arrived. Once more we were introduced and the ladies were welcomed to the party. We explained firstly that we had organised to follow up his offer to manage the National Stud and farm. He nodded and brushed this aside, as being of little consequence to the matters of our visit. Standing alongside the entrance was a raised dias covered, like his tent, in a brightly hued carpet. The Sheikh climbed up and beckoned us to follow. Once again taking a chair each we sat to face the area in front of the stables. I noticed that we were accompanied by three of the falconers with the hooded charges perched alongside. Mint tea was brought and the parade began. Grooms came out in pairs with their charges, who were walked past us, turned and trotted back for inspection. These were high class racing Arabs looking as though they had at least a sprinkling of Thoroughbred blood in them. Whilst the parade was going on, the sun was setting over the horizon, making a stunning backdrop for the show. As each pair was presented the Sheikh gave a commentary on their breeding and the performance of the older horses. This was passed on to us by an acolyte who spoke good English and had a deal of knowledge of the subject.

After seeing thirty or more horses of differing ages, two magnificent yearlings were led out. One was a chestnut filly, which moved with all the grace of a panther, the other a slightly bigger grey colt. This had the proud look of an eagle, matching that of his owner. Arrayed against the setting sun they presented a magical scene. As I sat admiring them, I was nudged by Dave. Turning, I found the Sheikh looking in my direction. He waved his finger at me and said something in Arabic. The interpreter told me that the Sheikh wanted to know which horse I thought was the best. My companion gave a laugh

"Now Charlie, you had better get this right or we might be going home tomorrow without you."

Thanking him for his help, I tossed a mental coin, and decided that the colt probably had my vote. Pointing to the grey, my relief was obvious as our host grinned and nodded his agreement. With that the show was over and we followed the owner off the dais. I for one was pleased to end there, whilst it appeared that I had made a good choice and could leave with my reputation more or less intact.

The next day we boarded a plane for Jeddah, where we were to pick up a British Airways flight home. It had certainly been a marvellous introduction to the Middle East. It was to be the first of many for me, but never again was I to experience the luxuries of VIP travel. My visits gradually deteriorated in style until I ended up in the public queue finding my own taxi to a local hotel. But whatever the circumstances none of them could cloud this first exotic visit to the land from which came the forebears of the English racehorse.

CHAPTER 9

Further Arabian Assignations (1970's)

The week after our return from Riyadh was hectic to say the least. Firstly we had to find our gang of young lads, then we had to arrange visas, passports, and book flights. The leader of the troop was to be one of the workers on the stud in England who had a lifetime's experience of working with his father on Newmarket studs. The second choice was a farmer's son from Dorset, who spoke in the broadest country brogue, such that we had a job to understand him at times. Still, the workers on the farm out there would not understand him whichever way he was to talk. The third member of the team was to be my eldest son, who had just completed his school exams and was waiting for a year to go to university. He was at that time passionate about the third world, and I figured that the world could not get much more third than working with the staff on the farm.

The farm manager on the stud in Berkshire was to go with the team and to be in overall charge of the enterprise on the ground. Dick was out of the old school and welcomed this new enterprise as a chance to relive the high days of the British Raj. Sad to say, that he, like the rest of us, was only too soon to realise our limitations when it came to impressing Saudi bureaucracy.

The initial party was made up by Dave and I to oversee the horse side, and James, a farmer from the West Country, who would help Dick get things started. Since Dave and I were due back in Kuwait that week, we were only to stay for three days in Riyadh to organise the takeover of the stud. We duly all met at the Saudi Airline desk to check in for the flight. It was like old times again as we lined up to board at the rear end of the plane. Memories of leisurely strolling up to the front end of the aircraft began to fade away. I was seated alongside an American who was working for an oil company. On explaining why we were headed for Saudi, he suggested that whatever contract we had arranged, we should add at least fifty per cent for the 'buggerment' factor. I laughed at this cynical view, but I was only too soon to understand what he meant.

We gathered our troops together, having just managed to get everybody through the customs. I had a minor hiccup when the customs official wanted to impound the boxes of worm medicine which I had brought out for the horses. He was convinced that I was smuggling some noxious drug into his country. Only after considerable arm waving and pointing out the pictures of horses on the front of the packet did he let me through. This was not as bad as when on a subsequent visit I was bringing some sheep dip from England and the official was determined to drink some to see if it was alcohol. In vain did I try to tell him that it was poisonous to humans. An American who was sitting by, reading the last of his copy of Playboy, which they were about to confiscate, told me to carry on and let him drink it. For the sake of international relations it was just as well that I was eventually allowed to take the dip through untasted.

We got everybody into a van and made for the office of our contact man. He handed us some money for horse feed and for our own basic needs, and directed us to a hostel outside the city, where we were to camp for a few days. The next morning we went to the complex to be greeted with delight by the chief stud man. Instructing him to organise some feed, we left the farm contingent to see where they were to start with the cattle. Meanwhile we organised the staff to herd the mares into the two large sheds so that we could catch them and dose them with the worm medicine. This operation tested our helpers to the extreme since none of the animals had been handled. I was pleased to see how willing the staff were once they got the message as to what was required of them.

By the time we had finished the dosing, a truck had drawn up full of alfalfa. The lads fell on this and handed it out liberally to the grateful mares. Thinking that we had completed a good morning's work, we sat down to have a snack on excellent flat unleavened bread. At this stage the local veterinary surgeon, an Indian, arrived and made himself known. He seemed surprised to see us there, but took me by the arm to see some of his patients. These consisted of a number of sheep, which were suffering from varying degrees of abscesses around their heads and necks. When I asked what he was treating them with, I learned that his only medicaments were even older than those with which I had started practice some thirty years before. I gathered that the Ministry stores had a supply of modern drugs such as antibiotics, but would not release them to him. I undertook to go the the store that afternoon and collect a number of drugs, which we might need. This I eventually managed, but it was like prising teeth to get them to part with anything.

I left Dave to see what could be done about the fencing and repairs to the stable doors, many of which owed their present upright position to copious lengths of string and strategically placed baulks of timber. Going over the cattle department I found the team there busy scrubbing out the milking parlour. They showed me the containers with that morning's milk. The contents were a rich brown, due to a heavy contamination with sand. Apparently this milk was sent daily to the King's palace for the use of the inhabitants there. It transpired that the only inhabitants to benefit from this were the racing camels. Once the cleaning up process was completed and the parlour was rebuilt the milk changed colour to the rich creamy look, which we associated with Channel Island cattle. Unfortunately this change was not appreciated and the camels were unwilling to drink this strange new mixture.

The next three days were spent fencing, scrubbing out mangers, and arranging for a farrier to come out to trim the feet, which had been neglected to the extent that some of the mares had toes like Persian slippers. While a lot of this was going on I was busy trying to establish whether the mares had been covered by the stallions and if so were they in foal. It appeared that nobody had a clear record of what the present situation was, so I could see that on my next visit I would have to examine the mares. Not a pleasing thought, since they were hard enough to catch let along examine. We managed to arrange for our team to move into a building on the farm, which had ample accommodation for them. We also obtained a four wheel drive truck for our use, so at least they could get to the shops and buy provisions. Dick bravely took on the job of driving, and hoisting a Union Jack on the front, he sallied off into town. At that time we did not know that the road to the farm was the main road to Jeddah. During the Haj when a mass of people went to Mecca, the road became like a race track and accidents were a daily occurrence.

Promising to return in a matter of days, Dave and I set off for the airline office in town to confirm our tickets for the flight to Kuwait. It was our first experience of this office and, as we waited patiently in a queue to claim our seats, it dawned on us that the system demanded that we push our way to the front or we would be standing there for days. Eventually armed with the tickets, we made for the airport and boarded a plane for Dahrhan. There we were to change on to a British Airways flight for the short hop to Kuwait. I was to make this trip many times, and on each occasion the sight of the white VC10 coming into land was a welcome breath of normality. Not only the thought of a large ice cold gin and tonic filled our minds, but also the visions of a deep bath on our arrival was a salutory treat.

Arriving in Kuwait we were met by Sheikh Fahad's friend, Rashid, who took us to the hotel. After a bath and general clean up, we were collected and driven out to the stables. I made plans to examine the mares on the next day as they had been brought back from the stud to the stables. The sick horse had thankfully recovered after being injected with the special drug, which had duly arrived from India. Shortly after we had been around the horses, Sheikh Fahad arrived and took us to his new racing stable alongside the race track. Compared with what we had experienced in Riyadh this was a different world. The stables were arranged in two facing rows of large boxes, each with its own insect destroyer. The sound of the zap as another moth hit the ultra-violet element became a steady rhythm, which in time was quite soothing. At the front of the stables was a large room with a television set and packs of cards. To this room it seemed half the men in Kuwait would come at about six o'clock and stay until at least eleven or later. It was to tax my patience on many occasions as I waited for somebody to take me back to my hotel in town. Since they started work in their offices at six thirty in the morning, I wondered if they ever got to see their wives or girlfriends. However Kuwait seemed full of young children, so no doubt the system worked satisfactorily.

The next morning I began to examine the mares in the company of Rashid's brother, who I had met at the stud on the previous visit. To my chagrin I discovered that most of the mares were in fact barren, and only five were in foal. Suggesting that I took some tests on the empty mares, which I could take back to England to examine, I innocently landed myself with a return visit to treat them. Sheikh Fahad was disappointed with the result and initially blamed the stallion that he was using. Consequently he asked us to find him a replacement to be sent out. Not only that, but he was keen to become involved with British racing and said we could buy him some yearlings to race for the next year. This was the beginning of a fascinating round of the sales, both at home and in America. Between us, Dave and I bought twenty three horses over a period of four years of which nineteen were to win races. The best was probably a horse which finished fourth in the Two Thousand Guineas, only to break a blood vessel in his lungs two days before the Derby when he was third favourite.

When I had finished with the mares, Rashid's brother took me to the souk in town. There I met his father, who had a shop selling clothes and cloth. He was by then in his eighties and had started his life as a pearl diver. This involved diving to extraordinary depths without any modern aids such as oxygen tanks. It was supposed to be a killer of an occupation, yet had clearly done this old man no lasting harm. The fact that one could still meet someone who had been part of an age old practice brought to mind how rapidly the country had progressed into such a modern society. Fahad had told me that, when a boy, his father had taken him shooting wolves over the site which was now occupied by the Hilton hotel. Since the hotel stood on the sea front opposite the British embassy, it was difficult to conjure up the idea of such a primitive land in view of the present state of this flourishing city. After yet another afternoon spent watching a football match, we returned home to consider our next moves in these two differing kingdoms. We decided that we must return within two weeks to see how the team were progressing in Saudi, and I would go on to Kuwait to treat the mares. During the interim we managed to find a suitable stallion, which was grey and resembled an Arab in all but parentage.

On our return to Saudi, I was glad to see that the mares had picked up unbelievably now that they were being fed properly. On the first night back I committed an unforgivable sin by destroying two emaciated and mangy Shetland ponies that I discovered hidden away in a shed on the farm. Only after doing the fateful deed was I told that they had been given to the royal family on a State visit some years previously by the Emperor of Ethiopia. I arranged immediately for them to be given a solemn burial on the farm and reported to the Ministry that they had grown tired of life and had succumbed to old age. Fortunately I heard no more about this, but my local colleague had some sleepless nights over the episode.

The farm workers had been busy since their arrival. The milking parlour had been completely rebuilt and a new milking plant was expected any day from home. Some of the paddocks had been cleared of rubbish and were ready to be planted with alfalfa for the animals. An irrigation machine had arrived and was awaiting a hose before it could be used. We believed that this hose had already arrived at the airport so I accompanied James to see if we could locate it. Sure enough when we got to the airport we could see the hose lying on the tarmac. We approached the man in charge to request that we could pick up our prey. Oh dear! This was my first encounter with officialdom and what my American acquaintance had warmed me of – the 'buggerment factor'. No, he did not believe that our package had arrived. On showing him the offending article, he doubted whether it was our hose. It soon dawned on us that only a handful of crisp riyals would convince him of the hose's credentials. With the offering of a reward all became welcoming and the hose was delivered to our truck.

The arrival of the now complete irrigation plant brought about a frenzy of activity from our team, and the crop was planted without any further delay. We could not understand why the stud staff did not greet the thought of a plenitude of home grown alfalfa with delight. It was only after the hose pipe had been severed at night for the third time did we realise that they much preferred to have the feed delivered from outside since that allowed them to remove sufficient each day for their own sheep. Promises that they could still have a quantity of the home grown variety stilled this first sign of insurrection.

The morning start on the farm caused some amusement in that there were five vehicles, including diggers and dumper trucks, but only one serviceable battery and that on the four wheel drive. So the first half an hour was spent with the jump leads trying to encourage the various work horses into life. Once everything was revving satisfactorily each member of the team leapt onto their allotted craft and began the day's work. While there I was told to board the digger and help clear the sand for drainage ditches. Since my skill as a JCB driver was not great this caused amusement and considerable frustration to the drainage party as I scooped up that which they had meticulously prepared on the previous day. I had the strange feeling that while they were quite pleased to see me, they were not unhappy when I left them for Kuwait.

My veterinary involvement in Saudi was limited to the general surveillance of the health of the horses and treatment of varying numbers of sheep, which seemed to suffer from an infection of the skin due in the main to the dusty conditions under which they were kept. I did have one coup when I was asked to visit the King's palace to examine some ailing falcons. Now, even my staunchest admirers would not have rated my skills at avian medicine very highly, so it was not with great enthusiasm that I viewed the birds. They appeared dull and listless with evident signs of diarrhoea. I could only think that maybe they were suffering from some form of worm infestation. As a result I said I would bring back some medicine on my next visit. Enquiries at home resulted in my obtaining a tube of pills which were guaranteed to remove any offending parasites from any sort of bird. These I duly passed on to the palace and awaited results. Somewhat to my surprise and certainly to my relief it appeared that the treatment had been successful and I was now number one vet at the royal palace. My colleagues were delighted with this approbation although I had mixed feelings which were soon to be proved correct.

On my next visit back I received a summons to the palace. This time camels were on the agenda. Would I please come and instruct the camel keepers on how to artificially inseminate the racing camels. I was assured that they had the necessary equipment, and a minion was sent off to fetch the prized possession. He returned with a cardboard box under his arm. From this he produced like a 'deus ex machina' an artificial vagina for the collection of semen from a pig. This was in itself an unlikely perquisite for a Muslim community, and not only that, it was I was sure, not a valuable asset for working with camels' reproductive capacity. However mindful of my elevated status in the eyes of the rest of our team, I assured the palace staff that I would go back to England and obtain both the required impedimenta for the procedure and (under my breath) that I would find out how to proceed with the operation.

On my return home, I decided that the best place to learn a little about how camels reproduce would be Whipsnade Zoo, where I believed that at least they had a number of the species. I duly phoned the zoo and told them of my request. They immediately invited me to come and see them. When I arrived, I was directed to the office, where to my surprise I saw the office girls passing pieces of paper from one to the other with sniggers of amusement. Asking the keeper what was going on, he remarked that I was not to worry, they were only running a sweepstake on how long I would survive when I began my task in the desert. He then enlightened me as to how dangerous a male camel could be when engaged and more importantly, disturbed, during his love making. Apparently, to make matters worse, camels copulate on the ground and any effort to collect their semen would entail me groping in the sand between the male and his inamorata. To make his point the keeper led me out to the camel run, where I was approached by several large inquisitive beasts, all intent on breathing their foul smelling breath over me. His only advice to me was that I should always be sure to wear a good pair of running shoes so that I could make a rapid exit if things got nasty as he was sure they would.

Leaving the zoo with dismay, I determined that for certain the sweepstake was not going to be won by anybody. Despite a sure loss of face I had no intention of moving from equines to the humped variety of mammals. I was quite happy to allow someone else the chance of glory in the palace grounds. I did subsequently learn that a renowned colleague of mine in Newmarket was later quite successful with the technique in another part of the Middle East. Whether the Riyadh camels of today are produced by this artificial system I do not know. All I can say is that I am still alive and in one piece.

The only other encounter of a veterinary nature in Riyadh was a request from our contact man that I should come and see his horse which his daughter rode and which had a large growth between its front legs. This sounded as though it would require an interesting but simple surgical operation which I felt was well within the compass of my Indian colleague and myself. I agreed to see the animal and he came to pick me up to take me to the local riding school in town, where several of the royal families kept their horses. We arrived at a broken down yard resembling a badly run secondhand car dealer's premises on the outskirts of London. It had been raining, not entirely unusual for that area, and the ground was a quagmire.

The proud owner led me across the yard, which was ankle deep in mud, doing his best to keep his smart cloak and best Italian shoes out of the worst of the mire. He had some difficulty in locating the horse, indicating clearly that this was not his accustomed venue. Eventually he pointed out a stable at the far side of the yard, where the animal was looking over the door. This was not exactly true, as what he was looking over was an old Fordson tractor tyre, which had been propped up against the door frame. No doubt that this was an effective means of keeping the creature from straying, but unfortunately it proved a formidable obstacle for my companion. A tractor tyre is no light weight, especially when one tries to push it against six inches of sodden sand. I am afraid that I had not taken to this man from my first acquaintance, as I felt his interest in our project was solely to ensure that his share of any takings would be as large as he could make it. For this reason I firmly pulled down my professional hat and left him to get me access to the patient. This he succeeded in doing, but at great detriment to his clothing as the tyre toppled back and knocked him over into the mud.

The growth was a simple fatty tumour, in all probability non-malignant and therefore a nuisance rather than life threatening. Still it required removal so that it would cause no further trouble when his daughter rode. I explained that we could operate on the horse if he could arranged to have it brought out to the farm. It would need to have a general anaesthetic as the position of the growth would entail having the horse lying on the ground to remove it. He said he was sure that the manager of the riding school, who was an American lady, could fix up to send it out to us the next day. After he dropped me back at the farm, I found my local colleague and told him of our projected operation. We then searched around for the necessary equipment, which fortunately would not be anything very specialised. He told me that he had the required anaesthetic for the animal, and went off to fetch it. On his return he produced a bottle of a drug, which had long since gone out of use in the field of anaesthesia at home. Thank heavens that I had been around when it was the anaesthetic of choice. At least I remembered the dosage and the effects.

We rounded up some of the staff to prepare an operation site. Finding some empty sacks, we had these filled with bedding from the stables and laid them in a square by the veterinary office. All being ready, we awaited the arrival of the patient the next morning. The thought of something out of the ordinary brought a large crowd to watch, and routine work came to a standstill. The appointed hour came, but no patient. We waited on, and after another hour I telephoned the office in town to find out what had happened. It transpired that the horse was ready for its departure but was evincing a marked dislike of its transport. Further enquiry revealed that this transport was in the nature of an open truck requiring the horse to jump up six feet to board the luxury means of travel. Seemingly there was no more satisfactory vehicle available and the operation would have to wait for another time. Reporting back to the assembled crowd, I felt like the producer of a well-advertised concert having to tell the expectant audience that the star singer had failed to turn up. Muttering disappointment they shuffled back to work. By the time I returned from England the horse had apparently been sold, I imagine, growth and all.

The remainder of my time in Saudi Arabia seemed to be spent in dealing with officialdom. We had persistent trouble in drawing any money from the Ministry of Agriculture to pay any of the staff, either local or our own team. The system in Arab countries is that anybody can walk into the office of either a Minister or even a member of the ruling family. There you wait your turn to speak to the owner of the office. This can take many days and a great deal of patience. On one occasion I called on the Minister of Finance, and while waiting I sat next to two men from North Korea, who were waiting to negotiate a building contract. I gathered from them that they had been waiting for ten days. Repeating this to a friend at home who dealt with the Saudis, he explained that that was why the Koreans obtained these contracts, nobody else had sufficient patience to wait long enough to get an audience to nail the contract.

Our visits were mostly to the Minister of Agriculture, a charming man who was an Edinburgh graduate. We explained our problems to him, especially that the farm seemed to employ ninety people, although we only saw the full complement on pay day. James, who came with me, began to get aggressive with the Minister and said that we had been trying to draw some money for the last two weeks without any success.

Further Arabian Assignations

The Minister held his hand up and smiled saying that he quite understood our frustration and he would give us a personally signed letter authorising the Financial Ministry to release the funds. In addition, we were to make a register of the employees who were present on a working day. Any extra men who turned up only to get paid would be moved to another place.

We thanked him and took the letter over to the Ministry of Finance with considerable relief. At the Ministry we were met by a senior man, whom I had seen before. He greeted us warmly and we gave him the letter. Reading it he smiled and came up with the dreaded word "*bukra*" - tomorrow. Worse still, he offered one of his few phrases in English – "no problem". How I hated hearing that. It meant in reality that there was probably a host of problems ahead, but at that stage he had not thought of them. Returning the next day, our cheerful friend directed us to a man on the second floor, who, he assured us, would come up with the cash. We climbed the stairs only to be told by this second ranking official that he had passed on the letter to his subordinate on the floor above. Up again we went to find our next target in a small office. Asking for the money, he looked at us with a blank stare. Explaining about the Minister's personal letter, he sighed and fished about in his desk drawer, where we saw the letter scrumpled up under a pile of other urgent orders for payment. So much for the importance of the Minister's letter. Taking the previous piece of paper from him, we made our way back to our first contact. Seeing us again, he decided that enough was enough, and led us to the cashier, who without hesitation handed us the money. Such was the state of bureaucracy in this rich but secretive country.

During our time in Riyadh we had devised plans to turn the National Stud into a show place to which foreign dignatories could be taken to be suitably impressed. However all our plans and decisions had to be passed through the designated authority at the Ministry. This particular person had never shown any interest in our improvements and had only rarely visited the farm. Since he was the holder of a university degree, he was considered an expert on all things agricultural, even though we discovered that his degree had been gained in Cairo for cheese making. It was apparent that he was happy to use the expertise which came into the country, but wished to take all the credit for any ideas himself. This unsatisfactory state of affairs persisted and I could see no advantage in my further participation. Thus ended my travels to Saudi Arabia. The team also returned at the end of the year, pleased with their work, but bitterly disappointed that they could not pursue their objectives of transforming the farm and stud to a useful research centre for agriculture in that part of the world.

Meanwhile, interspersed with my visits to Saudi I was still making regular visits to Kuwait. We managed to improve the fertility of Sheikh Fahad's mares, although the sandy conditions on the stud were not ideal for breeding horses. I came to know my employer much better over the next few years. I learned about his time in Europe, which amongst other things had involved him in joining the Royal Marines. He had an interest in all things military, and spent some time up on the hills above Israel during the Israeli-Palestinian war. He telephoned me one day to ask me to get him some insecticide for his fruit trees, which was contained in large yellow tins. On questioning him he told me that he had seen the Israelis through his field glasses spraying their fruit orchards with something that came from these yellow containers. I was unable to find such an insecticide, but managed to find a substitute which apparently worked just as well.

During my visits I was introduced to several members of the Palestine Liberation Organisation, who had been spirited out of Palestine to Kuwait. It was an unusual experience for me to be engaged in political discussions with these passionate men. Unfortunately they seemed to believe that I had special access to the ear of Margaret Thatcher, and they implored me to intercede on their behalf. When I explained that this was some way outside my role as a veterinary advisor in Kuwait, I was treated to a diatribe explaining to me that all the troubles in the area were due to the Balfour Agreement for which I must take some responsibility. My efforts to point out that this Agreement had been made at least six or seven years before my arrival on the planet fell on deaf ears.

Halfway through my time in Kuwait the war between Iraq and Iran began. Hearing of the fighting around Basra on the radio at home, I phoned Fahad to see if it was safe for me to come out. He laughed and asked what I was frightened of. I explained that as a coward I rated ten on the Richter scale. He assured me that all was well, and on meeting me at the airport insisted on driving me up to the Iraq border to watch the fighting. I thanked him for the experience, but from then on kept a wary eye on the horizon towards the battle area.

The animals on the stud, both brood mares and racehorses improved on the added supplements and changes in their diets, the racehorses winning a satisfactory number of the local races. However it became clear that what was needed was a resident veterinary surgeon who could provide day to day treatment of the mares. Sheikh Fahad managed to find a Jordanian who had past experience of working with brood mares and my job became superfluous, except for giving advice by telephone from home. So ended my visits to the desert, which had been educational and fascinating. The horses which we had sent out from England proved their worth, and the few ponies which I had obtained for the equestrian club gave a lot of pleasure.

The last time I was to see Sheikh Fahad was in Korea at the Asian Games, where he was the President of the Asian Olympic Committee. Sadly the Iraq invasion of Kuwait was to prove fatal for this ebullient man. There were reports that he alone of the Royal family was incapable of escaping the invading Iraqis, but another report indicated that he had died on his palace steps, firing an anti-tank gun at the approaching tanks. Of the two stories I am far more than inclined to believe the second version. Fahad was a trained soldier, who kept his own armoury of weapons behind a hidden door in the cellar of the palace. He had once bemoaned that he had forgotten to bring back a vital piece of armament from London. I offered to bring this out the next day but he laughed and explained that it was the breech of a howitzer and as such likely to be a little bulky for my hand luggage.

Fahad had been a man to enjoy all the good things of life, when I first knew him, but latterly he had forsaken such vices as smoking and had begun regular prayers through the day. This he explained was because his children were now teenagers and he must set them a good example. The war brought a sad end to what had been a happy period of my life. Not only did I lose a good acquaintance, but also all the work with the horses was destroyed overnight. It was reported that the invading troops opened the stable doors and let the animals run loose into the desert. Their fate can only be left to the imagination, but it does not paint a pretty picture.

CHAPTER 10

Debut into Driving (1970's)

It all began during my first year at the Veterinary College, when I had bet our instructor that if I took a four-in-hand harness into its component parts he could not put it together again. It was a bet which I had cheekily won and duly received my dues. Alas, after a period of some thirty years had elapsed, my defeated colleague was to get his own back with interest. During the intervening period we had become great friends and next door neighbours in practice. Sometime after I had retired from Lambourn he telephoned me to offer me a job, which he assured me would be enjoyable and interesting. He was correct on both counts although my initial feelings were more of misgiving than pleasant anticipation.

It seemed that the British Four-in-Hand Driving team were short of a vet for their journey to the World Driving Championships in Hungary and my friend had thought that as I had nothing else to do I might like to fulfil this role. True, I had plenty of experience with horses, but these were of the kind which were used to somebody sitting on their backs rather than perched up behind them on a noisy cart. For a start, one was going to deal with a team of four large, strong animals, each presumably with a mind of its own. Still I was not being asked to drive them, only to see to their health and welfare both during the journey across Europe and through what I supposed was a stressful competition. All in all it sounded a challenge and maybe even a chance for a new learning experience; therefore I cautiously accepted. I asked my colleague for some tips on how to proceed. His response was not to worry. All the horses were seasoned travellers, and anyway most of them would have some degree of lameness, so my chief task would be to persuade the competition authorities not to throw them out before they had a chance to show their paces.

So began a period of fascinating forays with the drivers over a period covering some four competitions as team vet and several more in the rarified atmosphere as a veterinary official of the FEI. My first initiation was at a cocktail party the night before leaving for the continent. This was to enable the competitors to meet each other and outline plans for the journey. It was clear that the drivers all knew each other well and I was introduced to each with a valediction that I would spare no effort in safeguarding their horses. The team was cosmopolitan in the extreme, varying from the husband of Her Majesty, (a keen and very competitive driver), a tycoon owner of a fleet of helicopters, a scrap metal merchant from the North of England and an obviously down-to-earth Norfolk yeoman.

Having been completely put at my ease by Joe, the Chef d'Equipe, a large rotund Londoner who was to be our leader on the journey, I returned home to fill a trunk with every known medicament that I thought might be useful to treat any unexpected ailment which my charges might develop. I persuaded Wendy to take me early the next day to the Mews at Windsor from whence the party were due to depart at four o'clock in the morning. When I arrived there was pandemonium with five large horse boxes being filled with horses and carriages, to say nothing of the sundry support vehicles and caravans. I unloaded my trunk and my few possessions and was helped to load them into a lorry by a strong hand, which I only discovered after they were safely stowed to have belonged to the resident of the castle. My embarrassed thanks were brushed aside, and I myself was loaded into the castle Land Rover for the journey to Dover.

We set off in convoy, more like Billy Smart's circus than a highly tuned competition team. The competitors were to follow in two days time by air in considerably more comfort than yours truly, cramped up in the back seat surrounded by some of the impedimenta required for the battle ahead. Behind us in the troop was an elderly, courteous gentleman from Switzerland. I had been introduced to him on the previous evening, but I was still unsure of his role in our motley assembly. He followed us serenely in a new Rolls Royce. Halfway to Dover I came to the view that I should make his acquaintance again on the ferry, since the accommodation in his car seemed considerably more commodious than that even in a royal Land Rover.

We arrived at the ferry terminal with a full complement of vehicles and waited while these were loaded into the bowels of the ship. I made an inspection of the horses and arranged for the ramps to be at least partially opened to allow some air to circulate around their heads. The lorry deck of a car ferry is notoriously hot and foetid. Fortunately the horses proved to be much more accommodating to this unusual form of travel than I had anticipated. Having made sure that my charges were as comfortable as could be, I made my way to the upper deck. There I was met by Joe, our leader and guide. My first task it appeared was to make my way to the purser's office to collect a bundle, which had been deposited by our sponsors. My surprise was only matched by my delight when I was shown a number of cases of the very best Scotch whisky. Arranging for these to be carried down and stowed on the horse boxes, I joined my new friends for breakfast. I greeted Joe with a happy smile and said something about the journey looking much rosier after my visit to the purser.

"Steady on," he said, "there is one case for each team and the remainder will be carried in my caravan for emergencies."

Asking what emergencies he expected, he laughed and suggested I should wait and see.

At breakfast I met the other members of the party. Apart from those directly responsible for the horses there were at least five souls involved in varying roles at the competition. A husband and his wife, who was to be one of the judges, were known to me by name as world experts in the field of driving. The lady was a byword in the equestrian scene as one of the most renowned whips. I knew her brother well from a few professional visits to his stud near Reading, although I had known him previously over some fierce encounters at opposite ends of the table tennis table at Wendy's house in our courting days. His sister and her husband proved just as good companions, restoring my equilibrium on many occasions by resorting to Mozart interludes on their tape recorder over a glass of remedial whisky in their caravan when events were proving even more harassing than usual.

The gathering was completed by the man whom I knew had been responsible for organising the big horse show at Wembley in the autumn. His role was as general factotum, comforter and friend to all. The group was completed by Joe's wife, shortly to play the most important part in the whole affair, and the companion to the judge, whose main job appeared to be to keep the couple and others replete with full glasses. I managed to find a seat next to our Swiss companion, Henry, and discovered that he was to act as our interpreter and personal vade mecum. In addition to his other accomplishments was an abiding love for horses, which he kept at his home in Majorca. His knowledge of horse driving was not extensive, but infinitely superior to mine. I tentatively asked if I could accompany him on the next stage of the journey. He told me that he would be delighted for company to act as navigator on the journey.

Decamping from the ferry at Zebrugge, the party made for a racing stable halfway between the port and the German border, where we were to spend the first night. Thankfully all the vehicles were still in their appointed places in the convoy, led by Joe as pathfinder. After a few miles, Henry was called on the intercom to go ahead to make sure the stables were ready for the horses. He accepted with alacrity and sped up the dual carriageway at what I supposed was the accepted speed in Belgium. Alas, after five more miles we heard the familiar siren of a following police car. Pulling into the side of the road, I waited for my chauffeur to either be escorted off to the nearest court, or at the best fined some phenomenal sum in Belgian currency. Two traffic policemen walked up to the driver's window and wished us good day with a broad smile. To my surprise they apologised for stopping us and asked if they could possibly see around the interior of the car. Their request was not based on a need to search us for drugs or other smuggled goods, but merely because they had never had the opportunity to look inside such a magnificent car. On my suggestion that they might like to drive us to our destination, they declined with a grin, intimating that they did not think they could drive as fast as was obviously Henry's custom.

Free from the clutches of the local constabulary we made our way to the racecourse. On arrival we were greeted warmly and I was taken to view the stabling, which had all been made ready for our occupants. We then awaited the arrival of the travellers. One by one the lorries pulled into the yard, and the horses were unboxed and taken to their stable. With the exception of one handsome grey mare, all had travelled well. The mare was showing very slight signs of 'set fast' or cramp from the long incarceration in the horse box, which was in fact a converted bus, the front of this having been made into living quarters for the driver, John, and his merry group of helpers. These consisted of his partner, Sue, her mother, and three lady grooms. I volunteered to give the mare a relaxing injection, although I felt that she would be fully recovered by morning.

It was my first experience of this happy team. I became to appreciate that they were devoted to their five charges, and the slightest abnormality would be brought to my attention. In truth they were so much part of the family that they cared too much for the four legged members for them to be risked in what could be a rigorous sport. Following my medical attention I was asked in to the living area for what was to be the first of many cups of tea. Mother seemed to spend her whole time over the stove, brewing up incessant amounts of warm sweet tea. Rejoining the remainder of the group, we were shown our overnight accommodation in the dormitory for the racing lads. A meal was prepared for us in the canteen. I retired to bed that night feeling that this was all going to be a pleasant holiday.

As morning dawned I was awakened by the smell of cooking bacon and eggs. As I have already said, Joe's wife, Anne, was to be of great importance to us and she had begun well by offering a splendid breakfast for all. The horses were then loaded up for the second stage, which was to take us to Bavaria. The grey mare, Aggie, was, I was relieved to see, now completely recovered.

We set off again with Henry allotted a position behind Joe's caravan. I received some good natured banter as I climbed into the Rolls. At least I felt that I had been accepted by the group. Our first stop was at the border into Germany, and here I made my first big error. At the border all the passports, including those of the horses, had to be inspected and a veterinary surgeon would have to make sure that none of the animals were in poor health. We pulled into the car park at the customs station and asked the whereabouts of the Ministry vet. Nobody could help us, but they were sure he was about. After half an hour I felt that it was up to me to take some action, so I walked off to view the waiting lorries. At the far end of the park I spied the back view of a man clambering up the side of a stock waggon. Possibly this was the man we were awaiting for I walked towards the truck and saw that it was full of sheep. Bidding good morning in my best and only German, I asked if he was indeed the vet in charge. He climbed down and introduced himself as Dr Springer. I in turn announced myself as the vet with the group of horse boxes, and asked if he could be good enough to come and inspect them as we had a long trip in front of us. Regrettably, I believe he thought that I was there to ensure that he did a thorough job. Walking over to our convoy he asked that all the horses be unloaded to enable him to inspect them. I had hoped that he would simply look inside each truck to make sure that the requisite number of animals were present. As I passed on his request to the drivers and grooms, I had a distinct feeling that they were not over happy with the intervention.

However the inspection went well, if slowly, until we arrived at one lorry load. The five horses were duly paraded in front of the vet, and I was handed their passports by the groom in charge.

"Nelson," I whispered, "there are only four passports."

"Oh, that is all right, the guv'nor is bringing the other one with him."

Fortunately one carriage horse closely resembles its companions, since one tries to get a team to match each other as nearly as possible. For the next few minutes the sharks who inhabit the car parks of racecourses with their games of 'find the lady' would have been proud of me. I shuffled the four documents sufficiently to confuse not only myself, but also Dr Springer. He smiled, shook my hand and said we were free to move on.

We quickly loaded up the teams and drove through customs into Germany. Leaving Aachen to our left we headed for the south. There had been some discontented rumblings amongst the lorry drivers about the slow speed, which Joe was setting. The Royal Navy had adopted a similar system with convoys in the last war - all to proceed at the speed of the slowest ship. Unfortunately, in our case the old bus had a maximum speed of forty miles an hour, and that downhill with a following breeze. As a result it was soon evident that at least two of the more powerful vehicles were intent on not hanging about. This despite the fact that they had but a hazy idea of our destination. Joe sent out a continual cry over the intercom for them to get back in line, but maybe his London accent was misinterpreted by the northern drivers, since they studiously ignored him. The language over the radio got stronger as the miles went by, but with no noticeable effect.

As we proceeded down the autobahn towards our next over-night stop near Wiesbaden, first one and then two powerful lorries overtook us. The drivers hooted their farewells on the horns and, I gathered later, gestured to their leader in something resembling a reverse Churchill V sign as they passed the red-faced Londoner. As five o'clock arrived we pulled off the main road to a small, rustic village in a picturesque setting below the Bavarian hills. Our target was a riding school, managed by a lady who had learned her trade in Somerset. The entrance was through a wooden archway and into a courtyard, which would have looked at home in the Austrian Tyrol. Immaculate flower beds surrounded a gravel yard. The stables were arranged in two long rows, facing each other. At the far end was a large wooden building containing a full sized dressage arena. The owner and her staff, dressed in jackets with the stable name emblazoned on them, welcomed us and directed our by now depleted entourage to a parking area behind the stables. The horses were unloaded and taken by the willing stable staff to their splendidly prepared boxes. To our surprise we found that five of the stables were already in occupation by familiar steeds. Only then did we realise that at least one of our rogue lorries had beaten us to our destination. The driver understandably was well pleased with himself, and announced that he was quite capable of navigating his charges through Europe without having to proceed at a funereal pace. It did not bode well for our commander's authority on the rest of the journey.

He explained that he had stopped for a tea break with the other miscreant, but had not sighted him since leaving the roadside cafe. After ensuring that the horses were comfortable I joined the others, who were busy unloading quantities of food from the freezer in one of the three articulated trucks. I think that only then did I appreciate that

Joe not only organised the travel plan, but had also arranged enough foodstores to feed the whole group for around three weeks.

I was to share a caravan with John, the show impressario, who proved to be excellent company with a fund of tales about those in the horse world who to me were only names read about in equestrian journals. We had just washed and changed for dinner in a tent, put up by some of the grooms and drivers, when we heard an almighty crash with the sound of tearing wood. Rushing round to the stable yard, we were confronted by our missing truck now adorned by the frame work of the magnificent wooden arch. Up front sat the bemused chauffeur and his elderly father, who clearly felt that his impending visit to his Maker had arrived. The general feeling of the awestruck onlookers was of amusement at the sight, tempered with sorrow at this insult to our very kind hosts. I got the horses out unhurt and indeed looking as though this was part of their every day experience. No doubt with their particular driver this could well have been the truth.

My admiration for our party grew by leaps and bounds as they removed the debris from the cab, and asked for tools and fresh supplies of timber. Despite the long drive of the day they worked for three more hours replacing the damaged woodwork and managing to restore the approach to something nearly akin to that which we had first seen. What it was going to cost the truck crew in extra drinks on our arrival at the event I dreaded to think. After a peaceful night the cavalcade reformed with strict instructions to hold their place in the parade. Before we could set sail our 'gatecrasher' had to be shown a back way out of the establishment, from which he could not further destroy our host's timber work.

Since the Hungarian border was closed to lorries on Sundays, we were to spend the night at another riding centre in the hills near to Vienna. As we reached the designated turn off the main road, Henry and I were sent ahead to reconnoitre the route to the stables. We negotiated a hairpin bend and climbed up an ever-narrowing road until we found our port of call.

"They will never get the big trucks up here before dark," I said dispiritedly.

Henry agreed, since he had been in great danger of scratching the immaculate sides of his car. We entered the courtyard to warn our hosts of the possible impending arrival of our troops. They assured us that their own horse box regularly managed the narrow road. With this encouragement we returned to report our findings. The drivers assured us of their skill and restarted their engines. To my misgivings, the 'gatecrasher' was the most confident of his ability to proceed.

Leaving the lorries to try their luck at the mountainous route, the remainder of the party drove up to the stables. We were met by our hosts, two men in their thirties, enthusiasts of dressage. They knew the UK well having bought a number of Welsh Cobs for their personal use. It was evident that the place was designed for not only teaching but also for demonstrations and conferences. Apart from the typical Austrian mountain chalet, there were a number of stables and a large covered school. Adjoining the house was a splendid dining area, already laid out for an evening meal for all of our party. We were taken on a tour of the buildings, and I took a look at the stable accommodation. There were a number of good sized loose boxes, and three long areas divided by swinging bales to accommodate those horses over and above the number to fill the boxes. I was assured by the company that the driving horses would have been used to being tied in stalls, separated from each other by the lengths of wood.

We were then shown the sleeping areas, which had been made ready for us. It caused some, I thought uncalled for, hilarity when it was decreed that Henry and I should share a large double bed in a loft over the stable. Since we had already spent so much time together in the car, it was felt that we were an ideal couple. The others were directed to various rooms. Two of the ladies were honoured when shown into a lofty double bedroom, which was clearly the main room of the chalet. They became puzzled as they made ready for bed as to why there was a large mirror suspended above the bed. A variety of suggestions were made, but it was felt best to draw a veil over the exact purpose. By the time that we had completed our tour of the premises the horses finally arrived. The lorries had eventually managed to complete the tortuous road with nothing more than a few rubs to the sides and two lost wing mirrors.

After dinner, Henry and I climbed the stairs to our palatial bed. Having argued over who was most likely to snore, we turned out the light. No sooner had we done this than we were aware of a crashing and banging below us. Obviously at least two of the inhabitants of the stable had taken a violent dislike to each other. Reluctantly I climbed out of bed and made my way down the stairs. Looking round the door I found two of the Hungarian greys conducting a fierce argument as to who was to have the more room between the swinging bales. I realised that they were much more accustomed to their comfortable partitions in the old bus, and further missed the ministrations of their kindly lady grooms. I managed to part the warring couple and decided that my presence was going to be necessary if Henry was to have any sleep.

After an hour perching on a straw bale I was relieved when Sue put her head round the door to ensure that her favoured horses were happy. I explained what had transpired and she laughed and said that the girls had put the horses in the wrong order. It seemed that Aggie and Pandur had never spoken to each other, one being a lead horse and the other a wheeler. I had already surmised that this meant that one was stationed in front of the vehicle and the other diametrically opposite in the van. Changing the animals round in the stall did the trick, at least temporarily. I agreed to sit with them for a bit and she would send one of the girls out later to take over from me. This worked satisfactorily, and at midnight I was relieved with a hot cup of tea. I returned to the bed to find Henry snoring like an asthmatic whale. I soon fell asleep and no doubt very quickly was rivalling my companion.

Since the border crossing into Hungary would be closed next day an early start was not on the cards. Leisurely we wandered down to breakfast and heard that a special performance of dressage to music had been arranged for us. It was to take place at midday allowing for the horses to be led out to stretch their legs. During breakfast Joe was summoned to the telephone. It was the British embassy in Budapest to say that they had organised for one border point to be opened specially for us at two o'clock. While I was pleased at the thought of getting the horses settled in their quarters at the competition site, I was sorry to miss the display. On hearing this news our hosts announced that they would put on their show immediately the horses had been fed. Thus I found myself in the school watching an entrancing display of High School work by two cobs to the glorious accompaniment of my two best-loved Mozart piano concertos.

Sadly we had to miss the lunch which had been planned to follow the demonstration. The horses were loaded up again and we set off once more with dire threats to anybody who departed from the convoy. It was no distance to the border as we approached the crossing point, warily eyeing the machine guns in the towers. It was my first visit to a communist country behind the Iron Curtain and I fully expected the worst to happen. To my surprise and relief we were met by a cheerful lady from the British embassy, who guided us through the formalities with infinitely less trouble than we had experienced on our entry to Germany. Alas, a count up of the vehicles disclosed the fact that we were one short. Needless to say it was our infamous 'gatecrasher' who was missing. Questioning the other drivers it seemed that he had been at the rear of the group, and had veered off at a crossroads towards the border further north. Superfluous to relate that was firmly closed. Frantic telephone calls from Joe to the driver managed to insist that he come back to the open crossing. Fortunately the officials agreed to await his arrival and one vehicle was left to guide him to Kescemet, where the competition was to be held.

Once again Henry and I were sent on ahead to supervise the stabling. The route took us straight through the city of Budapest, which we were seeing for the first time. While Buda was delightful and picturesque, high above the Danube, Pest was scruffy and dilapidated at that time. Worse still the signposts were rudimentary and shortly we were totally lost. Henry then proved his worth as a public relations man. Jumping out of the car, he hailed a passing taxi. Managing to explain that we wanted to find the road out towards Kescemet, he persuaded the taxi driver to lead us through the maze of little streets and out onto the main road. Having settled up with the driver, we wondered how on earth the others were to extricate themselves from the city. We need not have worried. The route that Joe had planned proved to be forbidden to commercial vehicles, and they were abruptly stopped by a posse of police. To their relief the police volunteered to guide them around the suburbs and out into the country. More phone calls back to the crossing point explained where they were to go when the errant truck arrived.

Henry drove on serenely through flat agricultural land, the road being punctuated by horse drawn farm carts, which studiously kept to the middle of the highway up until the very last moment. The set-up of these carts was unusual in that they were pulled by two horses, driven in tandem with both horses on the same side of the single shaft.

As we reached the attractive little village of Kescement we were directed by clear signposts to the stable area. This was in a large open-plan factory building surrounded by ample parking area. We were met by an official of the event, a young Hungarian vet, who was to organise the veterinary side of the competition. I introduced myself and asked if we could see the stabling. He led us into the building, which had been partitioned by lengths of high chipboard to allow sufficient area for each national team. Apart from rings in the wall and a manger to each horse, there was no separation of the horses from each other. Remembering my problems of the previous night, I said we would have to have some form of segregation of one horse from another. Sadly he told me that he had no authority to arrange for this, and his boss was taking the Sunday off. I walked around the outside of the site and noticed a large heap of wooden poles, about seven foot in length. These would have to do as swinging bales, but where were we to find a sufficient amount of rope to tie the ends to the metal struts supporting the roof? My new friend thought he knew where rope could be obtained, and unhappily departed to see if he could persuade someone to part with it. Again I said that we would give him all the support that he needed in standing up against his superiors.

Further investigation found a number of horses being walked around the perimeter of the stable area. I walked over to them with Henry, and he was delighted to learn that they were the representatives of his native country, Switzerland. Asking where their companions were, the grooms said that the owners were coming next day and that their lorry driver had returned to Switzerland. His early departure was partly explained later when the authorities firmly refused to have any lorries parked within walking distance of the stables. The Swiss had craftily got over this prohibition by leaving their truck immediately outside the stables and encouraging the driver to lock the driving cab and take the key back home with him. This ploy was improved on by one of our drivers, whose box was to be used as sleeping quarters for several grooms. He parked his truck by the side of the stable, removed a front wheel, hid it behind the straw and announced to the authorities that it had been taken off for repair.

By the time we had finished our investigations the bulk of our group had arrived. I broke the good news to them that they could not unload the horses until we had arranged some form of partitioning in the so-called stable! The grooms and drivers leapt into action with a will, and before many minutes men were clambering up and down the roof supports like so many agitated monkeys. They had just completed enough partitions for the British horses when the stable manager arrived. He looked aghast at our work, but two bottles of the Scottish nectar rapidly alleviated his anxieties. While we were putting the equine charges to bed and feeding them, other foreign teams began to show up. They viewed our efforts with approval and hastily made similar arrangements for their own horses.

Once the animals were safely installed we went off to find our own accommodation. This had been set up in a holiday camp in a park some ten minutes walk from the stables. The walk was one that I was to take several times a day. It was an unnerving stroll since on the other side of the road was a Russian army barracks, guarded by a tower in which sat two soldiers whose instructions were apparently to train their machine guns on any pedestrian walking past. It was like that feeling you get when proceeding through the green channel of the customs at airports, even if you have only got two extra packets of cigarettes in your case.

The next day was a rest day for the horses, who were led out, with the exception of one team, whose coachman had just arrived by plane from England. He was determined to harness up his horses and take them for some vigorous exercise in the adjoining park. This was viewed with horror by Joe and the other experts, and I was told, as the team vet, to ask him not to do this as the horses were stiff and tired after their long journey. He laughed at me and suggested that I did not know what I was talking about.

"If you think these buggers are tired you come up on the box with me and try to waggon them yourself."

Gingerly I climbed up with him. I had not realised the impression of height and insecurity one gets perched up like a sparrow on the narrow seat. Further, looking over the backs of four large horses was similar, I imagined, to standing on the bridge of a supertanker. The lead horses' ears were yards in front of my position. Before I could recover from my feeling of vertigo he thrust the reins into my hands, gave a flick of his whip over the leaders. They immediately plunged forward, nearly dragging me over the front of the coach. I grabbed the reins and tried to take a pull. It was as though I was on the losing side of a tug-of-war team. They set off at a good trot and my efforts to restrain them had no more effect than that of a fly.

"Now do you still think they are too tired for any work?"

I had to admit defeat, and to my relief he stopped the coach and I gratefully climbed down. My first veterinary effort was not a truly auspicious beginning.

On my way back I was met by one of John's girls, who asked me if I could go and look at one of their horses which was slightly lame. I was greeted at the stables by John with an excitable Aggie. He led her out and trotted her up. She was obviously lame on her right hind leg. She had unfortunately once again not approved of her makeshift pen, which did not favourably compare with her comfortable loose box home in Norfolk. I found that the source of the trouble was a tweaked muscle high in her quarters. I heard that one of our other teams had thoughtfully brought along a Faradic Stimulation machine. With this I set to work applying small shocks to the affected muscle. I believed that a further two applications should cure the trouble but as I was about to leave the area, I was approached by the Swedish Chef d'Equipe. He was worried about a big black stallion who was breathing fast and showing clear signs of considerable distress. His temperature was well up and I did not offer a very hopeful prognosis. Further enquiries elicited the fact they had made the trip from home without a stop, approximately eighteen hours in the lorry. This confirmed my fears that the horse was suffering from severe transport sickness. I dosed him with a hefty amount of antibiotics, and went to find my Hungarian veterinary colleague. Explaining the situation, I suggested that the horse would need transfusing with quantities of fluid if he was to survive. The doctor said he would call on his hospital colleagues to see to the unfortunate animal. Alas their efforts proved in vain, which proved to me the benefits of overnight stops during long distance road transport.

CHAPTER 11

Further Delving into Driving (1970's)

O nce all the contestants had safely arrived it was time for the World
Four-in-Hand Driving Competition to start in earnest. The first stage
was for the teams to make their acquaintance with the marathon course.

The marathon corresponds to the speed and endurance phase in
Three Day Eventing. The carriages are specially constructed to
withstand rough country and frequent battering against the obstacles,
of which there are about ten. These are built to prove the driver's skill
at negotiating tricky corners and awkward distances at speed. The
course builders delight in making these so narrow that to my
inexperienced eye there was no chance that four horses and a carriage
could get through them even at a walk.

While awaiting the start of the inspection I wandered across to
the famous bus to see if tea was on the boil. On my way over I was
called over by one of our team to watch the arrival of the last
country's group. These were the Russian horses, which had travelled
in an open army three ton lorry. The horses were tied in two rows of
five animals along each side of the truck facing outwards with a rope
slung loosely over their necks. We wondered where they were
planning to unload them since there was no ramp available. With
complete aplomb, the grooms unhitched the ropes and each horse
jumped nimbly down off the truck onto the tarmac. It was not so
surprising then that the Hungarians did not understand all of our fuss
about the stabling. Incidentally I never did get to see how they loaded
the animals up again after the event was over.

All the competition drivers and their support teams gathered in a
column of military four wheel drive vehicles. The ground for the
marathon was soft from recent rain and the soil, being sandy, was deep
in places. Those of the foreign teams, who had brought Range Rovers
joined in the fleet. I climbed up into Joe's truck to have my first view of
a marathon course. It was Joe's task as Chef d'Equipe to look at the

obstacles and to arrange for us hangers-on to be placed around the course on the day of action to signal back to him how the other competitors were faring at each hazard. We had only nine non-combatants, so it was decided that one innocent looking thatched pile around which the carriages were to be driven was so simple that it could be ignored. Needless to say that was the one which caused one of our team to turn over and to spill its occupants on the ground.

On the way around the course we had to negotiate a deep ditch. This proved impassable to all the four wheel vehicles with exception of John's car which drove straight through with no hesitation. The car was a small Subaru four wheel drive saloon, which had pulled his carriage from England. It was my first experience of these cars, which have now become so popular.

The following day saw the start of the competition proper. It began with the first inspection of the horses by the judges advised by the chief veterinary surgeon, a Hungarian. Each horse was trotted up to ensure that they were sound enough to begin the competition. This was my induction into gamemanship in driving. I had been warned at home that some of our group were possibly not as sound as they might be, since they spent their lives trotting great distances on hard roads. Sure enough, two animals in one team gave me cause for worry when I had asked for them to be pulled out before the official inspection. I mentioned my worries to Joe, who told me not to fear as he would lead the most obvious one for the inspection. This he duly did to the great amusement of the spectators. Suffice it to say that Joe was a large man, with not a very athletic figure. The crowd were laughing so much at his efforts that neither they nor the judges noticed the slight nodding of the horse's head. It is fair to point out that although not one hundred percent sound on the gravel drive, the horse was completely all right during the competition on the grass surface.

The opening part of the Championship was the presentation phase. This required four teams to present themselves around the ring, where the judges allotted marks for the harness and the polish on the show carriages. Each team had to walk to a new point round the ring, where they stood at attention for a further five minutes. To my amazement the stands were packed for this spectacle. I have heard people say that watching dressage is like watching paint dry. Take my word for it, those people have never watched the first element of a driving competition. When it comes to spit and polish the British are in their element and the result of the first day found us in the lead. This was only fair return for the hours spent by the grooms buffing up collars and traces to say nothing of the shining paintwork on the carriages. I should have said that four-in-hand driving is almost a national sport in Hungary, but this initial part was not considered so essential to them, despite their attire in costumes from the old Austro-Hungarian empire.

When I got back from this exciting experience I was accosted by a French driver. Could I come and see one of his horses with a touch of colic? The stress of the arena efforts had proved too much for his delicate digestion. It appeared that I was the only foreign vet at the site, and I could see that my time was going to be well occupied. A very different situation from that which rules today when there seem to be as many vets as horses at international competitions. Thankfully a simple dose of salt and liquid paraffin effected a complete cure without transgressing any of the international regulations on medication.

The second day was devoted to dressage, which demanded the coachmen to drive intricate circles around the ring in front of the four judges. This brought no further problems for me except when our own lady judge left her position in the box for a personal but unavoidable reason. Unfortunately when she attempted to return to her position she was stopped by the security police and refused entry. My efforts to help were of no avail and the language problem was only overcome when Henry was summoned to her aid.

The third day brought the much anticipated marathon. For this, each competitor was permitted to change his team of horses from the preceding day. I now understood why we had brought five horses for each group. I had believed that this was simply in case one horse should become lame or ill, whereas in fact the fifth horse was a specialist for the endurance phase. This meant that not only was he fleeter of foot but more willing, or more stupid, to lead his fellows at breakneck speed into unknown dangers in the obstacles. Gone were the shining harnesses and smart carriages. Tack was notable for its toughness, in many parts reinforced by strong rope. The carriages were built like tanks with solid steel sides and iron guards on the wheels. When I saw the Hungarians in particular hurling their vehicles round tree trunks and heavy posts with abandon I could see the necessity for these arrangements.

The carriages each were manned by the driver and two grooms, who stood in the rear to aid with the balance as they cornered at speed around each obstacle. In addition a referee sat up on the box seat alongside the driver. His job was to check that the true course was followed and that at no stage did the horses break into a canter. This may sound simple, but I can attest from performing the task with John at a competition in Norfolk, it is a terrifying experience. There is virtually no hand-hold to help in retaining one's equilibrium, and to add to the problem the referee is burdened with a pen, clip-board, and stopwatch to note down any contravention of the rules. It was interesting to see how the prettiest and best dressed ladies would vie to ride with one member of our team. In their ignorance they did not realise to what dangers they were subjecting themselves. On most occasions they would arrive at the finish ashen-faced and dishevelled.

At one particularly nasty hazard at this event the poor referee was decanted from his seat as the team galloped through a stream. The driver being loathe to lose any time sped on without him until he was able to retake his place somewhat out of breath as the carriage left the time zone of the obstacle.

For the British team the marathon went reasonably well but for the aforementioned spill, and two other refusals which entailed the grooms having to dismount to disentangle the horses, thus losing precious points. John, I thought not surprisingly, felt that his beloved steeds had gone quite fast enough and slowed up towards the end of the course, incurring time penalties. Since the weather had been warm, I felt that I should do something to alleviate any effects of dehydration in the horses. To this end I enlisted Henry's help to buy a plentiful supply of bicarbonate of soda to add to their drinking water that night. We decided that the supermarket in town would no doubt be able to provide the wherewithal for our needs. We went in and found a few small packets of bicarb, sufficient for two horses. Henry enquired from the manager if they had any more in store. I am sure he thought we were engaged in some capitalist ploy to remove the country's supply of this essential cooking item. However, he departed to see what he could find, coming back with handfulls of the small packets. Our arrival at the check-out caused great mirth to the local shoppers to whom Henry explained the reason for our strange need. Learning that we were from England they all began to shout and cheer, much to my embarrassment. When I realised that they were the unwilling hosts to their Russian masters at that time, it became clear that we represented something for which they longed, and I am delighted that before many months, they achieved a beneficent democracy.

My round of the participants was not too depressing; a few scrapes and bruises being the only casualties. A late evening trot up of our horses showed three slightly lame. These were given pain killing powders in their night feed - a ploy permitted by the rules at that time. Next morning I was pleased to see that all but one was sound enough for the judge's final inspection. The lame horse was substituted by a fellow member of his team. Although this was in fact a marathon horse the driver felt that he would manage to last the phase if he was put in as a wheel horse. We had finished the marathon in fourth place, but my companions were confident that we would move up in the cone driving. This phase, like the show jumping in Three Day Eventing was to test the recovery of the horses and coachmen from the rigours of the day before. Cones were laid out in pairs around the main arena, allowing merely a few inches for the carriages to wind their way between them. Five points were deducted for each cone dislodged. Our drivers did us proud and we finished in the bronze medal position behind the Hungarians and the Dutch.

All that was left now was the presentation of prizes, or so I thought. I had not reckoned with the lodging of objections by various dissatisfied teams. It transpired that Joe was a past master at such bargaining. An hour later however he emerged crestfallen at his failure to push our team up into the silver position. It was well worth a try, but he was unable to convince the appeal committee that one dressage judge had been more interested in a good looking lady in the crowd than one of our team performing in front of him. The resulting marks allotted to the competitor had made the difference between us and the Dutch in the final analysis.

The competition proper being over it was time for celebration of wins and drowning of sorrows. The Hungarians proved not only to be skilled horse drivers but also prolific drinkers. We were all summoned to their stable where a fiendish local drink called Barak was dispensed with no regard to drink driving laws. Their clear intention was to prove that they could drink all the foreign nationals under the table. This they nearly succeeded in doing, except that one or two of us faint hearted souls retired while we could still walk. In the evening John asked me to come round to the bus for a further drink as he had a favour to ask. I declined the temptation of another bout of alcohol, but a cup of restoring tea seemed in order. He had arranged with one of the Hungarian drivers to visit his stud next morning with the intention of buying an additional horse for his team. Would I mind coming with him to vet anything that took his fancy? This I looked forward to for I had heard a lot about the State breeding farms. As it turned out there was quite a formidable group who arrived at the Stud, including two other drivers, anxious to see what John was up to and how much a horse could be bought for.

We drove out through rolling country past a large lake, which was popular with the townsfolk of Budapest as a holiday resort. The Stud was much more extensive than I had imagined. There were over two hundred horses bred and trained there. We were shown into a long building where some eighty horses were tethered in stalls. These were in the main four or five year olds, about sixteen and a half hands high. They were the strong active types, which would have graced many a hunting field back home. The stud manager, our opposition of the past three days, was in charge of the whole operation, but took a chief interest in the breaking of the young horses. No wonder they were able to produce such efficient teams with so many to choose from.

Three horses were brought out for John's inspection. One had an ominous bump on its pastern, which looked suspiciously like a ringbone. The second was a big raw boned gelding, whose pelvis showed a marked deviation from the normal. The third, a five year old grey gelding, was an upstanding horse with considerable presence. This took John's eye and he asked if I could vet it for him. At long last a job with which I felt comfortable. I felt its limbs, examined its heart and eyes, and asked if they could exercise it for me. A saddle and bridle was fetched and the manager jumped up into the saddle. He trotted it round and then set off at a rare gallop so that I could test its wind. To me it seemed perfectly in order, so John asked if it had been trained to pull a cart. They laughed at this and explained that had been the first part of its education. A rally cart was pulled out of the shed next door and the animal was harnessed up. John and Sue climbed up alongside the manager, who disappeared into the distance at somewhat the same speed as he had achieved when riding it.

While the rest of us were waiting for them to return, the Hungarian asked if we would like to see one of the number performing a display. We all nodded our assent, and three horses were brought out and fitted with bridles. A small wiry man came out of the stable and sprang onto the back of one of them. He was then handed the reins of the two others, one on each side. As he walked away from us he climbed onto his feet on the back of the middle horse. Once up he urged the horses into a fast canter, then moved one foot onto the left hand horse and then his other onto the remaining outside horse. Thus perilously balanced he galloped in figures of eight in front of us, finally coming to a stop to receive the unstinting applause of the guests. It was the first time I had seen such a proficient display of balance and horsemanship. We were then told that he had learned this skill from the age of ten and to the best of the staff's knowledge had never fallen off.

A cloud of dust in the distance signalled the return of our horse buyer. John was now driving and well pleased with the horse. The haggling will now begin, I thought to myself. But a deal had already been struck on the drive around the stud. I believe the gelding changed hands for somewhere around one thousand pounds, a very reasonable price for a good horse anywhere. To the best of my knowledge he remained in John's team for many years, appearing at many shows such as Olympia, pulling the stage coach with his new colleagues.

The next problem was to arrange for all the papers to be collected and signed before we left for home the next day. This seemed a tall order for any country, let alone a communist state with all its red tape. Another surprise of this enchanting land was the alacrity with which a deal could be arranged for hard foreign cash. A government official was on hand to deal with the formalities immediately. A hitch occurred when John was asked for his passport, which he had thoughtfully brought with him. It transpired that this had become dislodged from his hip pocket during the hectic drive around the farm. Sue remembered a particularly deep ditch over which they had bumped, and a deputation was sent to see if they could find the missing document. It must have been a good omen for the horse when they found the passport at the side of the track by the ditch.

Leaving the stud to arrange to bring the horse to Kescemet, we went back to start packing all the gear into the lorries. Next morning we once again got into some semblance of a convoy to make our way back to the border crossing. This time it should have been plain sailing for the journey home and so it was, at least as far as the border. The customs officials checked all the lorries and horses and cheerfully told Joe that no horse could leave except for the new purchase, whose papers were in order. Once more the British embassy was called into action. After an hour all was sorted and we proceeded into Austria. Only when back in a Western country was Joe told that instead of ten carriages we now only had nine, since one of the drivers had done a deal with a Hungarian driver for his show vehicle. Joe's language became rich again, and the driver, who was returning by plane, must have suffered from very red hot ears. Since we had made an early morning start we were to drive straight to the riding school at Wiesbaden for the first night's stop. This worked out with no problems. On our arrival at the school, Joe telephoned the shipping agents in England to tell them that we had got one extra horse and one less carriage. This would enable us to get through Dover with no delay, or so we hoped.

The second day took us back to Aachen, where a final night's stop had been arranged on the outskirts of the town. Alas, Joe's navigation this time let him down. Instead of turning off to the arranged stopping point, the majority of the convoy drove into the centre of the city in the midst of the afternoon rush hour. Frantic calls were made over the various intercoms to try and find out where everybody was. Driving down the main street we saw to our horror John happily proceeding up the other carriageway, heading back towards the south. Queries as to where he was going resulted in his cheerful Norfolk twang announcing that he had no idea, but he had been diverted back by a traffic policeman. Joe did a U turn and eventually found our destination. Three cars and one horse box were already established there. As I climbed out I noticed a main police station next to our parking area. Foolishly I volunteered to seek help from the constabulary. I entered the large impressive building and found what appeared to be the duty officer with five or six shirt-sleeved police officials. Asking if anybody spoke English, I was met with a decisive negative. There was nothing for it but for me to try my more than limited German.

"Wir verlieren fier pferdewagon in Aachen." ("We have lost four horsesboxes in Aachen.")

This produced laughter and disbelief. I gathered that they were intimating that this was impossible and even if it had happened there was no way they could help. At this moment a fresh and more senior policeman came in the room to see what all the laughter was about. Thank goodness he spoke a little more English than I did German. He translated his underlings reply to my plea, and I had indeed got the gist of their meaning. Thinking of the size of the lorries and also about the questionable skills of our 'gatecrasher' I assured him that mayhem could arrive in the centre of town at any minute. No sooner said than done! Messages arrived at headquarters to the effect that all the traffic had come to a halt, and some idiot English horsemen were causing chaos to their normally ordered existence. Now action was rapid. Orders were flashed to mobile patrols to escort our lorries out of the centre. I pointed out of the window at the park to which they should be shepherded. Half an hour later all was restored and the convoy was fully assembled under Joe's command.

Surprisingly all the combatants reached the ferry terminal and arrived in Dover in good heart. We were met by the shipping agent with a long face. The customs would not allow our new acquisition into the country unless it could be quarantined in isolation for ten days. Varying ideas for this were put forward until somebody asked if Windsor Castle Mews would be a satisfactory quarantine station. At this the customs stood to attention and agreed that they could accept this. All that remained was for Joe to make contact with the Castle to see if they took to the idea of receiving a foreign immigrant. To all our relief this was agreed and the entourage proceeded back to whence we had started out some ten days before.

So ended my initiation into horse driving. I was to accompany the team on two or three more occasions to varying locations such as Holland and Switzerland. These produced their tally of problems, but by then I was well accustomed to the system of this engaging sport. Although not especially testing for my veterinary skills, it was great to be amongst some cheerful people who were motivated entirely by the love of the competition rather than by any monetary gain which has bedevilled other equestrian disciplines to a certain degree.

Further Delving into Driving

After the visit to Zug in Switzerland I graduated to acting as an FEI official at a further two events. In Hungary again I was appointed as the Foreign Veterinary Delegate with the responsibility of seeing fair play according to the rules. As an official I had a different view from that I had developed as a team vet. More emphasis was placed on ensuring the welfare of the horses. I had to approach the obstacles with an interest in the safety of the horses instead of learning how they might be negotiated. On occasions I had to remonstrate with the builders as to various dangers in their construction. This was not always accepted with entirely good grace, since they viewed their constructions with considerable pride. As an advisor to the judges I paid great attention to the 'gamesmanship' ploys that I had previously encouraged. It was wise to be wary when a team had five grey horses to present as it was not beyond bounds for them to arrange a quick swap of the horses and to try to present a sound horse twice, thereby keeping a doubtful animal out of the firing line. This ploy was usually accompanied by a flurry of whip cracking, all aimed to confuse the inspection party. The most important task was to ensure that all the horses were in a fit enough condition to begin the marathon obstacle phase. Prior to the start they had to complete a long journey around roads and tracks, which could prove a gruelling effort in often hot and steamy weather. The vet in the so-called 'ten minute box' has a most important job to examine each horse for lameness, harness rubs, and exhaustion. It is obligatory for each horse to rest for ten minutes before tackling the obstacles, and the grooms await them with plentiful supplies of water for both cooling their backs and for allowing a small drink.

I thoroughly enjoyed my part in this unique sport, which combines the elegance of the dressage, the Wild West driving of the marathon stage, and the nerve tingling excitement of the final cone phase. The sight of four splendid horses working in unison stimulates the admiration of all of us who derive so much pleasure from these marvellous animals.

CHAPTER 12
Mission to Milan (1980's)

For many years I had been struggling with an unfortunate allergy. Many people have peculiar reactions to shell-fish or grass pollen, both of which are inconvenient, but to varying extents avoidable. I, on the other hand, had been chosen to become allergic to the very creature from which I earned a living. Close contact with horses would result in my face and hands turning into a fiery, itching battleground. Routine dentistry with more than six or seven horses would mean an evening spent with my face buried in a handkerchief, wracked by convulsive sneezes.

An initial course of injections, self-administered over a six month period, had produced a satisfying immunity which lasted over fifteen years. As the immunity waned the memory of painful attempts to stab myself with a needle returned. My earlier enthusiasm was in no way matched by my middle-aged desire to avoid discomfort wherever possible. A visit to a specialist produced varying reactions. His assertion that a second course of injections would be inadvisable if not positively dangerous, was greeted with some heartfelt relief. His suggestion that tablets might alleviate the condition but would not cure it, was not one to be wholeheartedly welcomed.

I had threatened to leave the practice so many times over the years that my colleagues grinned disbelievingly when I again raised the subject. Aided by my pills, I decided to carry on until a specific date, when I would withdraw from the front line of active service. Thirty years in the same surgery was, I felt, sufficient an infliction on my clients and my partners to warrant a change of life. The appointed time arrived, and with considerable excitement as to what the future would hold, I hung up my scalpels and hypodermic syringes.

"Now," I told Wendy, "I can devote myself to the family and the stud."

She grunted with some disbelief at this statement. She, like many others, did not for one moment believe that I should be happy to be divorced from the world of horses and racing in particular. Despite the presence of thirty odd ponies and several thoroughbred brood mares at home, she knew that I would seek to creep back into the scene of action before many months.

How wrong she was! Rather than creep back in months, I was to charge back in weeks. I had no plans for the future when I drove finally out of Lambourn, other than vague notions of acting in a consultant capacity and helping any organisations which might be rash enough to consult me. I soon discovered that a consultant is only in demand in a ratio to the special knowledge which he has to offer. A jack of all trades, which is the lot of a general practitioner in the veterinary field, is without those qualifications which impress the client. Despite my inability to act as a specialist in diseases such as those affecting the middle ear or the deeper recesses of the small intestine, I was soon approached to offer advice on a number of different cases. The one advantage which I now possessed was the fact that as a retired practitioner I posed no threat to any of my colleagues.

The second discovery that I made was the seemingly endless number of committees that await the unemployed. The fact that I had time on my hands soon percolated through the horse world, with the result that invitations to join such and such a committee rained down in a steady stream. Feeling that I now had ample time, I accepted these with an alacrity which would have astonished me in previous times. Some people are born to be committee animals, others view them with a mixture of horror and disbelief. The latter was my first feeling as I was not, and still am not, one of nature's gifts to the procedure for discussing endless points of order and the minutiae of reports. Nevertheless, through the opportunities arising from various new commitments which I have since undertaken, I have learnt much and spent many enjoyable hours.

Mission to Milan

After one long session involving racing politics, I called in to cadge a drink off one of my bloodstock agent friends. Taffy Jones was a relatively new hand to the racing scene. Disillusioned by the humdrum life of a city accountant, he had joined forces with a cousin and was already on the way to becoming a major earner of foreign currency with his band of well britched continental businessmen, who were keen to make their mark on the British racing scene. His astute mathematical mind had quickly grasped the intricacies of the stud books and the form data both in England and abroad. As the trade in thoroughbreds became more international, it was imperative that agents and indeed vets should become more aware of the trends in racing in countries as diverse as America, Australia, Japan and Europe. An increasing number of people wished to have a part in the racing scene, not only as racehorse owners but also as owners of brood mares and of shares in stallions. The value of these constituted a trade of many hundreds of thousands of pounds.

Taffy looked up from his desk and welcomed me. Replacing one of the two telephone receivers he was holding, he told me to help myself to a jar whilst he continued to try to get his call through to Buenos Aires. Hoping that he could persuade his man there to buy the mare we had seen in Newmarket the previous week, he said that he had an option on a nomination to Northern Dancer in America for her, but unfortunately the option expired at six o'clock that evening. Realising the urgency of this high-powered deal, I poured myself a vodka and tonic and sat back to wait while my friend harangued some poor foreign operator in a mixture of Spanish, Italian and what sounded more like Gaelic. I soon came to understand that Taffy's command of foreign tongues was at best rudimentary. However after a couple of minutes he finally made contact with the South American tycoon. He replaced the receiver with a broad grin, saying that his client was mad keen to proceed. With that he

162

promptly dialled America to clinch the stallion deal. Since Northern Dancer was undoubtedly the most successful and sought after stallion in the world at that time, I knew that the nomination would be costing around three quarters of a million dollars.

Waiting for his call to go through, Taffy said that he had another deal going for which he wanted my help. Such is the closed world of thoroughbred breeding that this deal for well over a million pounds was completed in less time than I would have taken to order two bags of coal. Life was infinitely more high-powered than it had been in my college days when I had tremulously offered up to one hundred pounds for a horse at the old Elephant and Castle sales in London. Big business had entered the horse industry and with its arrival a lot of the fun and excitement had disappeared out of the window. But I realised that the transfer of such large sums of money meant that there was a greater need for people in my profession, since these deals relied to a major extent on the integrity and accuracy of the advisors' reports. In most cases the purchasers would not only be unlikely to have set eyes on their investments but also their knowledge of horses would be minimal. Many other professions marvel at the great level of trust which exists in the buying and selling of horses.

The deal completed, Taffy turned to me and said that he and I had a little job to do if I could spare two days of the following week. He was off to the yearling sales in Milan with William Green, a young trainer whom Taffy supported with the odd horse for a client. William was well known to me as he was based in Lambourn, having taken up training two years before, after spending several years as an assistant trainer. His initial start had been promising, but I felt that his chances of making a name for himself were not great since he was too nice to force horses on new clients. Rather than ingratiate himself with prospective owners, he would stay at home nurturing his garden and his few equine charges. My part in the operation would be to examine any possible purchases and to see that the other two did not get into any trouble.

I said that this seemed a fun outing and I would certainly join them so long as he organised everything and laid on the entertainment. I presumed that he was looking for some horses for his new client, Signor Minotti, for whom I had looked at three yearlings and two brood mares which Taffy had bought for the Italian in Newmarket. Both my friend and Signor Minotti now had high hopes of topping the owners' list in two years time. Agreeing with my guess, the bold agent said that he had been through the catalogue and had marked two or three horses, although the majority of the sale did not look prepossessing for English racing. It appeared that the client was very keen that we should go and see any likely horse and to buy it if it seemed sound. I left Taffy to continue his executive chores, and I departed for home with my instructions to turn up at Heathrow with my spyglass and squeakers at the appointed time. The next day Anne from the office phoned to give the flight time and to let me know that we were booked in at the Hilton and more importantly that Taffy had arranged for the three best looking girls in Milan to dine with us that evening.

Excusing myself from the daily routine on the stud, I told Wendy that I should only be away for one night. She looked disbelievingly at this, saying that at least when I was working I got home at night, whereas now I was more likely to be swanning around the fleshpots of Europe. The fact that William Green was coming with us gave her a modicum of confidence that we should have to behave. I assured her that she had nothing to worry about and that William was the soul of probity. She had obviously forgotten about some of the escapades when we went skiing together in Switzerland. On second thoughts perhaps she had not forgotten but was indulging in some wishful thinking.

Mission to Milan

The plane was due off at ten o'clock in the morning, and when I arrived at the check-in desk an hour before take off, William suggested we had time for a cup of coffee. Taffy was encumbered with every known newspaper, including two Italian dailies. I nervously asked him if he could really speak and understand Italian. William laughed and agreed that the papers were only for effect since he believed that between the three of us we could only muster about half a dozen words of Italian. At this I bristled since I reckoned to at least know my way down an Italian menu, although I would not welcome a long conversation with the waiter. The plane was called on time to the pleasure of our leader, who was confident that his arrangements would run smoothly. As we boarded he told me that he had spoken to his girl friend in Milan, she had fixed us up with two really sexy model girls for the evening whom we were to pick up for dinner. He himself was recently divorced and so available to good-looking girls. Encouraged by this enticing news we hurried down the corridor to the gate. As usual, the Milan plane was at the furthest slot in the complex. I have never seemed to be lucky enough to catch a plane which left from the first gate. This gate appears to be reserved for romantic places such as Singapore or Acapulco.

Taking our seats, we were informed by the captain that there would be a slight delay for a small technical fault to the main compass. A small fault indeed! When I dropped the compass off our yacht we ended up off the end of Bournemouth beach instead of in Weymouth harbour. Eventually, only three quarters of an hour late, we were airborne, only to be told that there was fog at Linata Airport and they could not accept us there. This was disconcerting to Taffy since he had arranged for Minotti's chauffeur to meet us. Sensing some incipient mutiny from his passengers, the captain offered a free round of drinks of which Taffy accepted a bottle of champagne, leaving William and I with a beer each.

It appeared that there was a fuel drivers strike in Milan so we headed for Nice to refuel. My suggestion that we should now decamp for the casino at Cannes was not greeted with enthusiasm by my companions, who were by now engrossed in the sales catalogue.

We eventually arrived in Milan and found that Signor Minotti had told his staff to send a car to each of the Milan airports, as nobody there had any idea where we should land. Four hours behind schedule I sat down in the car confident that from now on all would be plain sailing. I was soon disabused of this hope when we learnt that the driver could not speak one word of English and that Taffy's command of Italian was as primitive as we had feared. Fortunately 'The Hilton' is a universal word, understood by all races, so we booked into our rooms and had a belated lunch, and returned to our driver for the journey to the sale yard. The next problem was that Signor Minotti was away on business and had failed to tell the driver where the sale was being held. Looking again at the catalogue, which was a mine of information on the breeding and potential of the horses, nowhere did it mention the address of the sale. In vain we tried out odd words of Italian on our poor driver, but he merely shrugged his shoulders and turned his big brown eyes to the skies murmuring *"mama mia"* in despair. We were rapidly joining him in this state when William had the bright idea of asking a traffic policeman the way. We persuaded our man to pull up at a busy intersection in the city while Taffy jumped out with his catalogue and thrust it under the policeman's nose.

"Si, si, cavalli," he beamed, and ignoring the growing traffic jam came over to our car. A few rapid words and the chauffeur's expression changed from misery to ecstasy. He let in the clutch almost before the policeman could withdraw his head from the window and set off in the true tradition of the great Italian racing drivers of old.

Half an hour of fast motoring, accompanied all the way by expressive gestures with both arms as the driver gave us a detailed guide to Milan, brought us at last to the sale yard. Sending our leader on ahead to introduce himself to the auctioneers, the two of us followed him to the office. We were welcomed spontaneously, kissed on both cheeks and given large glasses of Chianti. Asking if we had everything that we required, they told us to let them know if there was slightest little thing which we might need to make our visit more comfortable. They clearly thought the big hitters had arrived with wads of lira in our pockets. Still, thinking of our evening's assignation with the girls, we all assured them that we were more than satisfied.

We left the office, overcome with the hospitality, and set off to examine the yearlings. Wherever we walked small Italians in tweed caps and tight fitting breeches followed us. If we so much as glanced at a loose box, one of them would leap in and bring out the inhabitant for our inspection. After a quarter of an hour of this treatment I came on an acquaintance of mine. He was one of the only two vets whom I knew in the country. He welcomed me with open arms.

"Charles, welcome to my country. We must have dinner and I will sing you more arias by Verdi."

I shook myself out of his embrace and explained that I was only there for the one day. The last time I had seen him was when he had regaled me with his off-tenor voice in a nightclub of doubtful reputation in San Francisco, and I was far from keen to relive that experience.

I said to the others that my friend, Gianfranco, could tell us if the bidding at the sale was only in Italian or if they also took the bids in English. I explained to Gianfranco that not one of the three of us spoke his language and we were not sure how many lira there were to the pound sterling. My songster friend spread out his arms in a gesture of sorrow. He explained that the bidding was only in Italian, but we should not have to worry as he would translate for us and make our bids to the auctioneer. It would, he said, give him the greatest pleasure to do this for his English colleague. I thanked him for his kind offer, explaining that in fact my companion, Taffy Jones, was in charge of the operation, and perhaps we would see how things turned out. I seemed to remember that the little Italian vet could get highly excited at moments of stress, and I feared that his enthusiasm might well leave our agent paying considerably more than he had bargained for. Promising to meet him for lunch the next day, I set off to catch up with my companions.

Of the four yearlings we had marked in the catalogue, two were so small that it was doubtful if they would ever carry a saddle let alone a jockey. One of the others was a well-made filly with a great walk. Her breeding was reasonable although not top class. The fourth horse was from an impeccable family, her relations having won in the States, England and France. She was a big plain chestnut with the longest ears I had seen on a thoroughbred. As she came out of the box she tripped and almost sprawled at our feet.

"A bit weak, isn't she?" said William eyeing her long raking back with some misgivings.

I had to agree, but said she might make a better three year old, since she clearly wanted a long time to build up her strength. Taffy was not so down-hearted and kept emphasising her good points. She had a lovely length of rein, plenty of scope and covered a lot of ground, he enthused. William merely muttered that she had nearly covered a lot of bloody Italian sand just then.

After a lot more to-ing and fro-ing between boxes, we decided that it would have to be one of our two fillies or nothing. Taffy went off to phone his client in Copenhagen and tell him what we had decided. The two of us felt that we deserved a drink to tide us over until the car returned. As I made my way to the bar, Gianfranco came rushing up and grabbed my arm. He introduced me to a man, whom he told me was from Naples and who wished to ask me about some of the yearlings.

Introducing himself as Carlo Peroni, he explained that he had heard of me in England and could I give him some help. How he had ever heard of me apart from the recent introduction from my medical colleague, I had no idea. Looking like the archetypal horseman, in his brown suit and smart tweed cap with a broad checked waistcoat, he handed me a well-thumbed catalogue. Could I say what I thought of the horses which he had marked with a cross? He would, I could be sure, pay me for any advice as his owner wanted me to act as his advisor, since the local trainers and vets were no good.

I was nonplussed at this remark as my Italian colleague was still standing at my shoulder. However he hastened to reassure me that he was not worried since he only worked for the breeders and did not give any advice on the purchase of the yearlings. Signor Peroni, he told me, worked for a rich Maltese owner. I quickly explained that I was employed by Mr Jones, but I would try and advise him about any animal in which we had no interest. Saying that he would give me a full list tomorrow, he walked off towards the stables.

Taffy returned and we made for the car park to find our limousine. The journey back into town was thankfully uneventful except for a detour for us to look at the most elaborate cemetery which I had ever seen. The driver carried on a rapid explanation in Italian, which Taffy translated as implying that all of the Milanese found their way beneath the impressive Doric pillars, regardless of party affiliations in life. The Communist lay happily with the Fascisti, the Signoras with the Signors. Since the main hospital was directly opposite the burial ground, separated by one of the busiest thoroughfares in Italy, I could see a certain evidence of sensible town planning. Once back at the hotel we had a discussion as to what we each thought the fillies would make on the next day. Our guesses varied from ten thousand pounds for the good looking one to maybe sixty thousand for the big awkward filly.

The calculator was produced to multiply our estimates into lira. The answer came to so many noughts that our international agent retired to the barman for a lesson in Italian figures.

At nine o'clock the three of us assembled in the foyer for our evening entertainment. As we passed the hotel desk, the receptionist stopped us. Did we know that there was now a general strike at both airports and that no flights would leave Milan for twenty four hours. We said we did not know and if that was the case we should wish to retain our rooms until the strikers returned to work. At least it would mean that we could continue our acquaintance with the delicious ladies for another evening.

We summoned a cab and asked the driver to go to the Via Maggiore, where we were to meet our companions. We threaded our way in and out of the traffic for ten minutes and finally drew up in a wide but deserted boulevard.

"*Trenta cinque,*" said Taffy with diminishing confidence. We pulled up outside the appointed number to be greeted by a series of large green shuttered doors of a warehouse. Not one light was to be seen from the upper four stories. William laughed, intimating that Taffy's lady must be a nightwatchwoman and hoped that her friends were not furniture removers. The party organiser got out of the cab and banged on one of the shutters. The sound reverberated down the street, but no sign of life emerged. Looking around he saw a large red bell push on the wall. As he walked up to this, the cabbie fell out of the cab and seized his arm.

"*No, signor. Polizia, polizia!*" he said in horror at the thought of his fare summoning the flying squad. By now both William and I had joined in the search. Walking round the corner William shouted that he had found a door bell. By the time that we had returned to the taxi a small door opened between two of the shutters and an extremely elegant blonde girl hurried out. Taffy embraced her and brought her over to where William and I were standing. He introduced her as

Marjorie. Then looking slightly apologetic he broke the sad news that she had been unable to persuade her friends to accompany her, so we were now to play gooseberry for the evening. So much for our night of bliss! Swallowing our disappointment we made for what turned out to be a splendid dinner in a restaurant which was patently the favourite of the most affluent gays in the city.

The next morning we arrived at the sale in good time to find ourselves seats on the rows of benches around the ring. The auctioneer began by reading out the conditions of sale. At least that was what we supposed he was doing, since in addition to talking in very rapid Italian, the loudspeaker so totally distorted his words as to make them incomprehensible to all of his audience.

The first lot in which we had a passing interest was number eight in the sale. A big strong Canisbay colt out of a Habitat mare. I had guessed that it would have fetched about twelve thousand pounds in England, based on its pedigree, being by a stallion which raced successfully for the Queen and out of a mare by a leading sire of brood mares. The bidding opened at "cinque mille" which was one of the few numbers I could recognise. The bids rose quickly in half millions although I could not see anyone raising their hands. All the time the auctioneer kept up a steady harangue which would have done justice to an American tobacco salesman and gave a vague idea as to where the bidding had reached. Without warning he stopped, turned to his assistant and the animal was led out of the ring. I looked over the shoulder of my next door neighbour and saw that he had written thirty three million on his page. Rapid calculations with Taffy indicated that the colt had been sold for twenty one thousand pounds. It did not look as though horses were going to be cheap in Milan.

William and I sat on and watched varying types of yearlings pass through the ring. Meanwhile, Taffy went off to phone Signor Minotti with the news that prices were higher than he had anticipated. Only by overlooking my neighbour's notes could I tell whether an animal had been sold or not. At long last the lot before our selection came into the ring. This brought that ominous surge of onlookers who throng the sale auditorium when a high price is expected. So many clustered around the auctioneer that genuine bidders become eclipsed. I saw my friend Gianfranco move to a vantage point opposite to where we were sitting. I lowered my head in case he should try to join in the fun on our behalf.

Taffy had returned and was lighting a cigarette - not in itself remarkable except that he never usually smoked the devil's weed, preferring the Havana type of smoke. By the time the excitement was over he had got through three and was coughing busily. The filly entered the ring, looking even plainer than she had on the previous day. The bidding started at ten million and there appeared to be plenty of interest for her as she soon stood at thirty million lira. Taffy nodded his head at the auctioneer, who seemed relieved that we had at last entered the fray. Bidding went steadily on and I nudged my companion to see whether he was still in the contest. Nervously he whispered that he thought he was involved but his limit was fifty million and he was not at all sure where the price had reached. William and I both thought that the last bid was forty million. Taffy waved again and to my dismay Gianfranco bid another half million.

"Good God," I muttered to William, "do you think he is bidding for or against us?"

William laughed and said he had no idea but he was quite sure that Taffy was lost. At forty nine million the bidding paused. Our man nodded once more, but immediately the little Italian capped his bid. Fifty million was now reached and that was sufficient for our party to cry enough.

"That's over forty thousand pounds and you two don't even like her!"

We climbed down from the stand and made our way to the bar. Taffy looked at William and said that as he had liked the other yearling, he could go and try and buy her for twenty thousand pounds, but as far as he was concerned he had suffered enough of taking the locals on in their foreign tongue. Not only was the language a problem but it was impossible to be sure what the last bid was. With that he decided to have one more walk around the stables. As I followed him there was a shout from the gate attendant. Simultaneously a grey colt shot through the opening, trailing its lead rein, and dodging the crowd like a wing three quarter, headed for the car park. As we watched its flight, a boy in ill-fitting breeches and a man in a familiar tweed suit came around the corner in hot but fruitless pursuit. As he saw me he stopped and asked if the English doctor had noticed the horse. I agreed that I had and waved in the vague direction of its line of escape. He then wondered if I thought he would be good to race or was he too big. Explaining that all I had seen was a flash of grey as it sped by, but its very speed could indicate that it might win a race.

Leaving the boy to recapture his charge, Carlo Peroni took my arm and breathlessly decided that he would leave the grey to somebody more fleet of foot. This seemed a wise choice since the colt had chosen to leave us all for good. Handing me a piece of paper with numbers on it, he asked if I had seen any of those lots. I glanced at the catalogue and realised that I had seen none of his selections. With that he hurried me to the yard. We began at one end and visited almost every other loosebox in the yard. I have never in my life seen such a motley and varied collection of horses. Most of them were tiny, but he assured me that his owner only wanted little animals. They had between them every known variety of conformation defect. Some had legs like corkscrews, others hocks so bent that their hind hooves nearly touched their fore ones. One was so nervous that its own attendant was unwilling to enter its box. Two others were completely disdainful of leaving the safety of theirs, and several others were patently not keen to return to theirs once we had seen them outside. Our tour around the sale yard left behind it the effect that a cyclone could have had. Stables boys and girls were left bemused after their employers had urged them to show their charges to the English doctor, only for my guide and I to rush into their box and then out and on to the next one.

I eventually narrowed Carlo's list to six from its original thirty odd. Pinning him in a corner of the yard, I asked exactly what he was looking for and how much he had to spend, since one or two which I had liked and had brought to his attention had been dismissed as being too expensive or not the type he wanted. He then explained that the trainer, who would have charge of any horse he bought, could only train small, light framed horses. Anything of any size would not stand for his rigorous methods. Carlo admitted that two million lira would be his top price, but he would rather stop at one and a half. Realising that he was trying to buy racehorses for less than one thousand pounds, I told him that I had possibly been too fussy, since I had been thinking of them rather in the light of animals which we would have been trying to buy for English racing. With horses, as with most other things, you tend to get what you pay for. The difference between one and fifty million lira represents a fair margin in conformation and breeding. I tried to console him with the thought that many cheap horses have turned into good racing propositions. However they had to have their wheels facing the right direction and sufficient room inside their bodies for a good engine, which was more than could be said for most of his selections.

By the time that we had completed our pilgrimage, the day's sale was ending. I found the other two leaning disconsolately on a rail. My supposition that we had not succeeded in obtaining a horse was answered by our agent saying that even though William had bid ten million over his orders he had still failed to buy the filly. William defensively grumbled that he was not to know that the auctioneer was still taking bids from him while he was only trying to light a cigarette. If the damned fag had not burst into life, heavens only knew what price he could have paid. We might have ended up taking home the most expensive animal of all time. I told them about my lightning tour round the stables and suggested that we hurry off before my new found client returned for an encore. With that we made for our driver, who once again gave us a tour around the cemetery on our way back to the hotel.

"I do believe that the wretched man wants us to book our plots here," said William as we cruised past the serried ranks of head stones. Once back at the hotel we decided on a quiet dinner on our own. It didn't seem as though our esteemed agent was as successful at organising female company as he had led us to believe.

The next morning dawned with bright sunshine so the other two were keen to have one more look at the sale before catching our plane home at lunchtime. This time I approached the ring with caution in case Carlo should be seeking a return match. I had only been there ten minutes before he sighted me, and asked me to see just two more horses. The first was a nervous bay filly which was so back at the knee that it seemed as though her front legs had been put on the wrong way round. The other was a small chestnut with a calloused fetlock joint. I asked the lad to trot it out for me, and it set off up the yard looking for all the world like Hopalong Cassidy. I advised Signor Peroni that I could not agree that he should buy either of these offerings. His face fell as he told me that he had already bought them that morning. I tried to reassure him by telling him that no doubt he could find somebody to take them off him, to which he replied that his trainer liked them and felt they should go a long way. I grinned back at this and suggested that perhaps he should then buy them himself and then take them a long way away, preferably out of the country.

I managed to disengage myself from Carlo and left him to try his luck again. Seizing my party I persuaded them that we should see the new sports complex before we returned home. We drove back to the enormous stadium where Inter Milan Football Club are based. Walking onto the ground we felt exactly as the early Christians must have felt when forced into the Colosseum along with the lions. We tried to picture the vast concrete stands filled to overflowing with the screaming Italian football fans, who must seem to those in the tiny playing area as an engulfing tide. From there we entered the impressive new trotting racecourse with its ultra-modern stands, which made Ascot look like a point-to-point course. It was sad for us flat racing enthusiasts to realise that trotting accounts for nearly two thirds of continental gambling. The immense sums of money available in this sport mean that every possible amenity can be installed for the devotee.

At two o'clock, three exhausted and disconsolate people climbed into the plane for the flight home. I at least had made a new acquaintance, who was to pursue me relentlessly during the coming months. Resulting from this encounter I made many visits to the Italian shores. My Italian improved, as I am glad to say, did my client's success for I was able to buy the man from Malta some decent racehorses. But the great romantic myth of Italy still has to be unveiled for me. As a country it seems to be populated with clerics and celibate ladies.

CHAPTER 13
Sallying to the Sales (1980's)

S hortly after my expedition to Milan I was invited by Taffy to join his Agency, chiefly to act as a veterinary advisor. Since the Italian trip had been enjoyable and even at some stages hysterical I accepted this offer. All that I could bring in the way of clientele was my Maltese friend, who dealt solely in cheap second hand stock. Hopefully I could improve on this by finding some more affluent individuals with a deal more ambition in the racing scene.

I was given a desk in the basement of the smart offices in Mayfair. However since my first task was to obtain and learn to operate a computer, I soon moved up to the nerve centre on the ground floor. To this room gravitated many of the racing personalities of the day, mainly I am afraid for a free drink in exchange for the latest nugget of gossip. Our new computer, which was the state of the art at that time, was christened Fred, for reasons which nobody could understand. Whether it was my lack of comprehension as to what Fred could do or could not do, I don't know, but Fred spent an enormity of time in his own special hospital in Epsom for repairs to his internal organs. Despite not ever truly mastering this piece of the new technological age, I managed to get the details of the majority of the horses then in training into his somewhat contrary memory. From this we could extract at the touch of a switch the history of any horse for which there might be an enquiry. Quite why we went to such elaborate and painstaking efforts when there were perfectly adequate form books published weekly, I am not now sure. However this gave me the feeling that I was now part of the Agency world. With this fund of up-to-date information we could scan the sales catalogues and annotate them with all the recent information.

Our first public outing was to the December breeding sales at Newmarket, for which Taffy had thoughtfully rented us a house in Exning just to the north west of the town. Called the Dog Kennel it suited us well, and became a centre for entertaining during the period of the sales. Deals were regularly done after a good dinner with a plentiful supply of port, only to be forgotten the next morning. Our third member was also called Charles, which caused some confusion. As he was, like Taffy, well over six foot tall, he had the authority to be Charles and I took the soubriquet of Charlie. It was Charles' main task to look after the commissariat, whilst I was the drinks dispenser.

I had been to the sales in Newmarket for many years, acting as veterinary consultant for our clients in Lambourn. This entailed looking at numbers of horses and performing what could only be a perfunctory vetting of them prior to them reaching the sale ring. Some of the agents would rush up and ask the nearest vet to look at a yearling seconds before it was due in the ring. One particular agent was a menace for this. On one very cold day he came to me and asked could I examine a colt to see whether he had been equipped with the requisite number of testicles. Now horses, like many people, are notoriously coy about allowing their nether regions to be felt. On this occasion the subject was a big fresh chestnut colt, who made it very clear that my freezing hand was not to be placed anywhere near his hind end. I managed to have a quick feel as he was plunging around just outside the parade ring. I was fairly sure that I could feel what I took to be a pair. The agent duly bought him in the ring and next day told me that he was already on his way to Brazil. I wondered for several weeks whether I should receive a strong letter from the Brazilian purchaser questioning my ability to count.

At this December sale we joined the busy throng of breeders studying catalogues and having numbers of mares and foals led out for their inspection. It is recognised that there are far more jockeys in the stands on a racecourse than ever get to ride a horse; similarly at sales the mere spectators greatly outnumber the serious buyers. We had three orders for mares and one for a foal. The latter I always have enjoyed seeing. Knowing how much they can alter from one year to the next makes their purchase a challenge but equally a lottery as is evident if one studies the returns at the yearling sales the following year. Pinhookers, those who buy foals to sell next year as yearlings, are to my mind the bravest of gamblers. Year after year they can be seen bidding prices equal to those fetched by yearlings in the same ring only two months previously. They must be mad, is the annual cry, but still they carry on spurred on by reports of the few which have shown maybe one hundred per cent appreciation. On this occasion I bought a bay colt foal for a friend of mine who was trapped at that time in hospital. Buying it for fifteen thousand pounds, it looked to me as though it should make a useful racehorse. Unfortunately it grew like Topsy and developed an unprepossessing walk. Its return as a yearling for my friend was not auspicious for my career as it made eight thousand pounds. To my eventual relief, but not to my friend's, it turned out to be a successful racehorse, running until it was eight years old and winning eleven races.

My partners bought two mares on my advice, since I could find no glaring faults. On the second last evening Taffy and I saw a rangy Mill Reef filly out of training, which did not seem to be much in demand. Acting entirely on the spur of the moment, with a liberal dose of Dutch courage from the bar, we bought her for thirteen thousand pounds. I awoke the next morning to the realisation that we had spent a major portion of the company's funds. As soon as we got back to the sale, we were accosted by a good judge who offered us a profit on the animal. I was all for taking his hand off, but Taffy decided against, arguing that if such an expert wanted her, we would be well advised to keep her for breeding. That decided, I phoned Wendy to warn her that we had a new arrival on the stud. The next year we sent her to a stallion in Ireland, which had superb breeding and a very successful racing career behind him. Regrettably that was the end of his prowess, as he proved to be a poor begetter of winners. The foal was not a prepossessing animal. As one of my Welsh friends would have said, "Boyo, there are hundreds like him." Towards the end of that year to my amazement we had a good offer for both mare and foal. With relief I saw them depart, but it was with mixed feelings that I saw that in subsequent years she bred four winners, two of them in minor stakes.

Sales embody a peculiar band of horse folk, who cannot resist the excitement of seeing class animals passing under the hammer to those who believe that they can afford them. To be part of this circus even in a small way is an education and a pleasure which I would willingly pay money to attend. Assiduously, you mark your catalogue with comments that cannot be shown to anybody else for fear of libel or worse being proved totally wrong by the horse's subsequent achievements. I have never had the courage to look back on the previous year's remarks. The few horses which I can remember frequently defied my comments, such is the mystery of racing. It is one of the spheres where swans can descend to lower levels of bird life and vice versa.

The excitement and wonder of the sales was never more evident than at the July yearling sales in Lexington, Kentucky. The three merry partners felt that we could not afford to be absent from this annual event, so tickets were bought in the business class of British Airways to Chicago and on to Lexington. Collecting ourselves at the Heathrow check-in desk we were joined by two acquaintances. They had no tickets, but seemed oblivious to this lack. Walking up to the desk they asked for George, who appeared to be one of the superior officials of the airline. Leaving them to their problems we went through to the duty free. Only when we boarded the plane did we see our friends again, taking their seats in the first class accommodation. "It is all a question of knowing the right people," was the response to our enquiries.

Arriving in Chicago we eventually persuaded the immigration authorities that we were not intent on causing trouble in their country, but in fact might leave them some of our money. We had only one order and that was for a brood mare, which was not in the sales, but on a stud in Maryland. I discovered that one of our superior travelling companions, a trainer, also had no orders to buy anything but when I met him in the bar on the last day of the sale, he told me that he had been offered five yearlings to train next season. All were owned by different widowed ladies, no doubt impressed with his smartly polished shoes and immaculate clothing.

For our part we were to stay with a lady who regularly visited the UK and at that time had a farm at which she prepared horses for the sales. Her husband was a partner in a veterinary practice in the town, and from him I learned of the long hours which he worked. I was pleased that I had resisted the offer some years before to leave England and settle in Kentucky. The money no doubt was plentiful, but the work would have killed me.

We shared our lodgings with two high-spirited Irishmen, one of whom I had known as a promising vet in the west of Ireland. He was destined to become well known in wider fields as a big time buyer of high class racehorses, and even more so as the only vet in history to have a Derby winner named after him. The second companion was already an acknowledged expert at breeding and selecting horses for the track. Our paths had crossed some years before when he bought a yearling of mine. It was an eye opener to listen to them discussing possible purchases. It was certain that anything they cast their minds on would be a first class specimen. Their courage in committing vast sums of money on untried stock astounded me. A half share in a foal by Nijinsky for several million dollars was but one of their ventures. That particular colt brought them a handsome profit when re-offered as a yearling the following year. I would not have had a wink of sleep for the intervening period if it had been my money.

My first entry to the sales paddocks at Lexington was accompanied by awestruck fascination. Some three hundred of the best bred horses in the world, all looking immaculate from the attentions of their hard working grooms. The boxes were laid out in rows with wide alleys between each row for the horses to be led out for inspection. At the end of each alley the sales company had provided tanks of ice with plentiful supplies of Coca Cola - not my favourite beverage. After an hour of walking around the horses in unbelievable heat and humidity I soon discovered a special taste for this previously disliked drink. At that time it was unusual for yearlings to be produced as if for a horse show. Our hostess, who had a number of choice lots for sale, had spent her youth in the show ring, so she was able to steal a march on the other vendors. It was not long before this custom spread across the water to our home sales. The problem which struck me was that the heat was having an adverse effect on the horses. It was difficult to persuade them to walk out properly, they clearly felt as enervated as did those inspecting them. I soon discovered that the more advanced vendors had arranged for an extra box to be at their disposal, where they dispensed stronger drinks than Cola. I met pina colada for the first time, as well as the local mint juleps. This enabled you to keep up your strength for what was a very long day - or perhaps it made one less discriminating.

Like all sale rings, rumour spread quickly about various horses. One of the fillies from our temporary home farm was being accused of having a dodgy fetlock joint. I went to look at her and could find nothing amiss. I duly set about countering the rumour with the contingent of British buyers, and I was pleased to see that she was bought to race in England for a good price, and even happier when she won two Group races. The various vendors set up boards advertising themselves above their allotted boxes. Alas, a partner of mine from home was assaulted by one of these as he walked underneath. The heavy board falling straight on his head, he was quickly carted off to hospital for x-rays, which fortunately showed no lasting damage. It proved that you needed a strong head to work in Lambourn.

In the eighties the rules of *Caveat Emptor* still ruled when buying horses. What you saw was what you bought. The vets could check the eyes, hearts and any obvious deviations of the limbs. The general use of radiology, endoscopes for peering down the respiratory system was unheard of. Today the wretched animals are subjected to a battery of diagnostic tests. Whether these enable one to pick out the best racehorses is very debatable. For me the first impression still is by far the most important indication of a horse's future potential. Very few successful racehorses have not had that indescribable hint of class. They always said that Arkle, without doubt the best chaser seen in my lifetime, had the look of eagles. If a horse does not look as though he knows he is good, he probably is not.

As I have said previously, I rarely remember the comments which I have scrawled in my catalogue, but I do recall looking at one well-bred and enormous colt, destined to make a fortune when his turn came to walk around the sale ring. I posed a question on the page of my catalogue: "Do they sell a cart for him as well?" They should have done so, as that might have been his metier since the racecourse was clearly not his chosen arena. One of the sad things about sales today is that the trainers who will have to look after the horses do not always get to choose their own purchases. As a result, agents examine the lots and eliminate any with what might be future problems. This results in many animals which have a small deviation from the normal being discarded. Many so-called limb abnormalities, will be of little consequence when they are put to racing. Experienced trainers recognise that a slight turning in of the fetlock joints will not cause later disasters. Similarly close attention is paid to the conformation of the hind legs. In my experience horses will race well with all sorts of peculiar hind limbs. The front ones are the ones which keep my profession in business.

To return to this sale, inspections over, we went to the sale ring for the auction to begin. Unlike the haphazard system at Newmarket, where bidders and spectators can find a seat anywhere in the magnificent arena, Keeneland Sales are conducted in a building resembling a high class cinema. Rather than the horses being paraded around a centre ring, the animals are led in one by one to stand on a raised platform underneath the auctioneer. A further strange sight to me was the pre-parade ring, which in America is under cover behind the sale ring. But even stranger was the fact that bidders can wave their catalogues to a spotter standing at the back of the rostrum. On one occasion I was fascinated to watch a party of bidders waving their bids of several million dollars for a horse, which had passed out of their sight, against another party whom they could not see. This certainly added to that which was becoming in my eyes, a visit to fairyland.

We had decided to arrange the whole excursion in style, so had booked our seats in the auditorium. Before each aisle of seating stood a spotter in smart evening dress. The man who encouraged our side to bid was a splendid character called Charlie. He carried out his task with all the fervour of a Manchester United fan yelling on his home team to further effort. One felt pangs of guilt if one was not obeying the imprecations of Charlie. The bids were sought by the auctioneer in the hectic style which I associated with tobacco auctioneers. It took some time firstly to realise that the figures being shouted out were not what had already been bid, but the next bid that was being asked for. This might not seem of great importance except that the prices being bandied about were in tens or even hundreds of thousand dollars. An actual genuine bid of three hundred thousand dollars would leave the auctioneer to shout out three hundred and fifty thousand dollars. I soon came to the conclusion that in some basement below the sale ring were two or three men rapidly printing dollars, such was the hysteria with which vast sums of money were rained in on the collection of livestock. Once again I wondered if I had done the right thing in giving up practice. If owners were so readily prepared to spend their fortunes, equine veterinary practice must resemble mining for gold.

For me the magic of Keeneland Sales was more than matched by the magic of Kentucky itself. Driving myself around the district, accompanied by the ever present country and western music on the car radio, I visited many of the famous stud farms. The very splendid sight of the miles of white painted rails around the paddocks of Calumet Farm, which greeted you on first arrival at the Bluegrass airport, was mind boggling. In those days, the Arabs had not yet built the magnificent studs in Newmarket, and the very size of the farms with their huge purpose built stud barns was truly a sight at which to marvel. As I called in at various farms on my own, I was amazed at the helpful attitude of the farm staff. One morning I drove into a palatial office to ask if I might catch a view of the fabulous Nijinsky. To my surprise I was welcomed with a cup of coffee and the stallion man was summoned to take me out to the great horse's paddock. He led me into the field, caught up Nijinsky and held him proudly for my benefit.

The rigours of the actual sale were interspersed by evening partying at different farms, who held gatherings aimed at entertaining prospective buyers and also at outdoing each other. One particular annual event was held which matched the best that Las Vegas could achieve. One night the theme was based on the circus. I happened to follow a sheikh from the Middle East into the farm. He was greeted by the host, who welcomed him in by offering him a ride on a camel, little realising that at home he had a fleet of racing camels which he had ridden since childhood. The cabaret consisted of the elderly, but still highly amusing, Bob Hope, followed by a well known blind pianist. The final act to my delight was none other than Cleo Lane. Clearly not a name to conjure with in the States, the audience continued to chatter during her opening offerings. However I was pleased to note how silence soon descended as her magical voice overcame their indifference.

Outside the entrance was a gas balloon, anchored to the ground by a steel rope. Finding that the basket, hovering about twenty feet above us, contained at least five well lubricated gentlemen from the UK, fruitless efforts were tried by some of our compatriots to launch them into the stratosphere above the Kentucky landscape.

During further visits to the sales, we moved our centre to one of the hotels in town. Needless to say the bars were filled to capacity by Europeans drowning their sorrow at failures to buy selected lots, or celebrating successes. One of our first duties was to seek out big Charles to appoint him as superintendent of the drinks department. Lexington, being in a dry area, would allow no sale of alcohol on Sundays, so Charles was despatched to the supermarket on Saturday to obtain adequate supplies for our team. On a subsequent visit with Wendy we stopped for a night on a Sunday at a local hotel in western Kentucky. I said to the waitress that being the Sabbath I did not expect a drink. She replied that I had no chance on any day, since that hotel was in a dry county.

One evening at dinner the gathering was disturbed by the arrival of the local sheriff, armed with the obligatory pearl handled set of revolvers. He marched up to the table next to us, and grabbed a well known English agent by the collar to drag him off to the town gaol. He was only persuaded to desist from this dastardly act by the combined efforts of all the other diners. It appeared that the previous evening he had been keeping bad company with a lawyer friend from home. Speeding back to the hotel in a fairly inebriated state they had been stopped by the local constabulary. Managing to escape their clutches by pretending not to understand the American language, they fled home. Alas their hired car was tracked down, and the lawyer spent several unhappy hours cooling his ardour behind bars.

As I have said, one of our few prearranged deals had been to sell a brood mare to a client. This mare was stabled at a farm in Maryland. So the day after the sale found our team in the company of the English vet back at the airport. Driving round to the private aircraft park, we skirted the Arab's personal jumbo, known as the 'Flying Carpet' to those trainers lucky enough to join its passenger list. I may say that the relief on the faces of vendors when it taxied into Lexington was always great.

We climbed into a six seater plane and headed for Baltimore. On arriving at the farm we found the mare ready for us. She was a strong deep-bodied chestnut, a stakes winner on the track and the dam of two useful horses. I left the vet to complete his examination and willingly accepted the offer to view the stallions, who were kept in a large barn. This was more like a throne room than a stable. The area between the boxes was carpeted in luxurious Turkish ware. The boxes were teak with polished brass fittings, and the bedding was prime straw. When I saw the chief occupant, I could well understand the reason for such elegance. I believe that the presence of the fantastic Northern Dancer was the high point of my visits to the sales. A small, but powerful chestnut, he exuded majesty even though he was by then an aged gentleman. Arguably the greatest stallion of this century, certainly so from the stream of high class progeny to race in Europe, his services at that time were in such enormous demand that he could command a fee of many hundreds of thousands of dollars from mare owners anxious to have one of his sons or daughters.

Sallying to the Sales

Having received a favourable report from the vet who was acting for the purchaser, Taffy phoned him with the good news. The deal was completed, and we made tracks for home. During the sale Taffy had managed to sell an Argentinian a share in an up and coming American stallion for three hundred thousand dollars, which valued the horse at an amazing twelve million. All in all we felt that our journey to Kentucky had been well worth while. For me it was an exciting view into a hitherto unimagined world.

Some years later Sheikh Fahad of Kuwait decided that Dave Dick and I should make an expedition to Lexington to find several yearlings. We were to fly over to Washington by Concorde, which was itself something to look forward to. Meeting up at Heathrow we were introduced to a lady who was deputed to look after the VIP's. She instructed Fahad to make himself known to the staff at Washington. This would save the hassle of getting from the international airport to the internal flights. To my chagrin Fahad would have none of this when we arrived, but insisted on lugging his large suitcase himself across the busy alleyways from immigration to our flight. Dressed in an old T shirt and grey flannels he certainly did not resemble a Very Important Person.

After finding our rooms in the Hyatt Regency we caught a taxi to the sales. As we intended to buy at least three horses, this meant that Dave and I had to look at all the horses. The big buyers usually employ somebody to tour the studs prior to the sales to weed out those they consider of no interest. This greatly reduces the leg work at the actual sale. Unfortunately we had to do this for ourselves. We soon realised that Fahad was not looking for the same type of horse as we were. Instead of searching out likely winners on the UK tracks, he was more interested in animals which vaguely resembled Arab horses in conformation. Further he wanted to buy only greys, which limited the field considerably.

We narrowed the possibles down to around fifteen yearlings, none of which should prove very expensive. I fell for a big chestnut colt, which by no stretch of the imagination could be taken for an Arabian. After much persuasion Fahad agreed that we could bid for it. When its turn came to be sold, Dave and I took our seats and began to wave our catalogues, much to Charlie (the spotter's) delight. The colt by Graustark, a son of Ribot who was one of my favourite sires, was knocked down to Dave for two hundred and fifty thousand dollars. Much pleased I returned to the hotel, only to wake up that night full of worries as to why it had been so cheap! Daylight brought the realisation that with VAT and transport it worked out at well over one hundred and fifty thousand pounds in English money. I devoutly hoped that it would win some races. In fact it did manage to win two amateur ridden races as a three-year-old. Not a great bargain, but Fahad seemed pleased enough with the result.

Besides the chestnut we bought two grey colts, selected by our client. Neither of the two inspired me too much, although they both fitted the bill for Fahad since if successful racehorses they would make just the sort of stallion he wanted for his mares in Kuwait. One did win several races, and was fourth in the Two Thousand Guineas at Newmarket. Since he was bred to stay further than a mile, we had hopes of the Derby for him. The ground at Epsom was for once soft from repeated rain, which would suit our horse well. Once again I was to wonder why we bother with the wretched animals, they manage to let you down so readily. The day before the big race the trainer breezed the colt to freshen him up for the contest. What did he do but break a blood vessel, which ruled out the chances of him even making the start? Following this catastrophe he was sold to the States, where they were allowed by the rules to race 'bleeders' under the influence of Lasix, a drug reputed to stop the propensity of breaking blood vessels. Sad to say in this case, even the wonder drug failed to help.

The third colt proved to suffer from that condition only too common amongst racehorses. It had more than its fair share of the 'slows'. I believe that I could have run faster up the gallops. The horse did nearly win a novice hurdle at Taunton, but the jockey failed to remember that the hurdle at the entrance into the straight was the final one. Waiting behind the leader, intending to jump past him at what he thought to be the next and last hurdle, he was beaten by half a length. Since this was not really the purpose for which the horse had been bought, I managed to sell him to a friend as a stallion in the Hunter Improvement Scheme. I am glad that he has been successful in this role, and is now living about half a mile from me to remind me of my visit to Kentucky with Sheikh Fahad.

The journey home from the sales with Fahad was not without incident. Once again we were to fly back on Concorde. Arriving at the international airport, we were ushered into the Concorde lounge, only to be told that there would be a delay as the plane had developed a mechanical fault. They were flying a replacement in from New York and so Dave and I passed the time by playing poker with two leading English trainers and a well known television commentator, who did some promotional work for British Airways and thus was entitled to first class travel wherever he wished. Why could I not find such a job? I was delighted that our domestic games of poker enabled me to fly home richer than I started out. On the flight with us was an American girl with a gorgeous tan and long auburn hair. Her arms were the bearers of not one but two magnificent gold bracelets. Dave nudged me and bet me fifty pounds that our Kuwaiti sheikh would escort her home from Heathrow. I am afraid to relate that I promptly lost some of my poker winnings. On disembarking, Fahad carried her bag and disappeared off to London in a hired limousine.

My final visit to Kentucky was to the autumn breeding sale. I was to buy a mare for a client for whom I had previously helped to buy some yearlings in England, one of which managed to win two Group races as a two year old. We bought a bay mare, but when I sent in my account for the commission, he told me that another agent could buy for him without any extra charges. This was the deciding factor for me that I was not really cut out for the job of a bloodstock agent. Taffy had regrettably come to the same decision since we had failed to persuade anybody to employ us to manage their studs, which was the main object of my presence in the firm. We parted on very good terms, he to manage the horses for another Arab, and I to return to more familiar veterinary scenes. Yet it was an interlude which I would not have missed for the world.

CHAPTER 14
Korean Kerfuffle (1980's)

After leaving practice I was persuaded to join the Veterinary Committee of the International Equestrian Federation, based in Switzerland. The FEI, as it is widely known in its French translation, deals with Show Jumping, Three Day Eventing, Dressage, Driving, Vaulting and Endurance Riding. The latter two disciplines fortunately did not come within my compass, as they represented totally unknown worlds to me. I was dubious about this undertaking, since all my previous experience had been involved with Thoroughbred racehorses. However, I felt that perhaps the two areas of competition were not so far distant. It was to turn out to be an intriguing interlude in my life.

Besides drafting the Veterinary Rules for competition, which did not differ markedly from those I knew from the Jockey Club in racing, vets were responsible for overseeing the welfare of the horses and the prevention of unlawful medication at competitions held under the auspices of the FEI. This entailed the presence of national veterinary surgeons at these competitions as well as one vet from a foreign country to ensure impartiality. It was in this role that I was to visit many diverse and interesting places. My visit to Australia for the first international Three Day Event to be held there is described in another chapter.

My most exotic and worrying commitment was to come when I was invited to officiate as President of the Veterinary Commission for the forthcoming Olympic Games to be held in South Korea in 1986. In their wisdom the Olympic Committee had decided that this was a suitable venue for all the competitions except the winter Olympics. Alas, they had not considered that the Koreans had little or no experience of horses let alone organising the most important event of the four year cycle for those involved in the disciplines concerned. Naturally enough the world's best horses and riders take part in these Games and they are rightly anxious for the well-being of their mounts. Since it was plain that the local veterinary forces had no past experience of the requirements necessary to run such a competition, the FEI felt that they should appoint somebody who had received a baptism of fire in more usual equine countries. For this reason I found myself appointed to organise the equine veterinary side of the meeting.

My experience of the Far East was minimal, and I viewed the enterprise with considerable trepidation. All I knew was that there was a small racecourse in Seoul and a few native ponies on an island off the mainland. Not an encouraging beginning. We had determined that at least there were no nasty infectious diseases, which could affect horses in the area, but that was only a start as a confidence booster to the owners of prospective competitors. In order to get a rough idea of the likely problems, I set off for Korea three years before the due date for the Games. This was to be a far from auspicious start. I was currently involved in another research project for the FEI which required me to visit the university in Sacramento in California. I decided to combine the two trips, and duly arrived in sun-drenched California for my meeting. The flight to Sacramento from England required me to change planes in San Francisco. The journey out was trouble free, but problems arose on my return flight to San Francisco, where I was to catch a plane to Seoul. The plane for the short hop was a small six seater, and the crew sensibly suggested that I put all my luggage in the aft stowage area. On arrival at the international airport they assured me that the baggage would be transferred to the United airline desk for me to collect.

I had but half an hour between flights and as I checked in, I inquired about my luggage only to be met by a bland smile and a shake of the head. No, they had seen nothing of my two cases, but if I would board the plane they were sure the items would follow. Only slightly reassured I took my seat. As we took off down the runway, I checked my pockets. Yes, there were my tickets and my passport. But no, my wallet with all my money and credit cards had been stupidly lodged in my overnight bag. Hoping that the airline staff would be as good as their word, I settled down to work out what I had to do on my arrival. The flight was to stop in Japan to pick up more passengers. Imagine my despair when we were told in the transit lounge that the plane was not fit to continue its journey that night.

Unfortunately I had no possibility of letting my Korean hosts know of my delay, but I trusted that they would discover the new arrival time next day. This I am pleased to say they had, and I was met at the terminal by a courteous Korean veterinary surgeon, who worked for one of the international drug companies and, thank heavens, spoke perfect English. He explained that my first assignment was scheduled for that morning when I was to address the local vets to explain some of the mysteries of the FEI rules. The meeting was to be held at the veterinary clinic at the new Olympic site. This turned out to be a modern racecourse with some two hundred stables and excellent facilities, including lungeing rings and exercise areas. The clinic was well appointed with a modern Japanese x-ray unit and a new operating table. Unfortunately I soon discovered that as yet this had not been used, since none of the vets had received any training in surgical techniques. I began by pointing out that they were to be hosts to some of the most valuable horses in the world, and that we must arrange for at least two experienced surgeons to be on site for the Games. I felt that I could not take the responsibility for a horse suddenly suffering from an emergency colic or worse still for one with a fractured leg without a good back-up team. This appeared to be greeted with some relief by the assembled audience.

I ran through the rules as best I could, and finished by asking for any questions. Immediately one of the vets at the back of the room held up his hand and said,

Korean Kerfuffle

"Please when do we get to shoot a horse?"

I presumed he was asking about any serious injury on the endurance phase of the Three Day Event, and I hastily assured him that if any shooting was to be done, it would be done by myself or one of the attending experts. I could imagine the enthusiasm which would be shown should any animal fall at a fence. Rapid despatch was not on my agenda. Instead I would have to try to organise transport to convey any injured steed from the site back to the hospital. Since the cross country course was some twenty miles away along narrow roads, this might, and in fact did, take some planning.

Once the talk was completed, I was delighted to meet with a young Korean vet who had spent some time with me at home in order to learn the rudiments of equine practice. The FEI in their wisdom had originally arranged for him to join the veterinary school in Berne for this purpose. However the basic object was not achieved, since the vets there conversed in German, or even worse in Switzer-Deutsche, neither of which tongues did he understand. He told me that he had been appointed as the local vet to the Veterinary Commission for the Games. Tragically between my first visit and that a year later, he was struck down by cancer and had to forgo his appointment. I am pleased to say that despite this he was able to attend the Olympics three years later in an advisory capacity. He put down his recovery to treatment by old Chinese remedies. This was my first experience of this ancient branch of medicine, and many conversations with the Koreans convinced me of the value of these techniques, which seemed illogical to somebody trained in Western medicine.

When the morning's talk was completed and a preliminary tour of the new site had shown me that at least the stables and exercise areas would pose little trouble for a major influx of foreign horses and their various attentive followers, I was taken for my first Korean meal. I was no expert at the use of chop sticks and my feeble efforts caused considerable amusement to my hosts. The diet was also totally strange to me: spicy and enriched by the Korean staple food, *Kimchi.* The latter was a concoction of pickled cabbage, which had been allowed to ferment in earthenware jars for, I felt, longer than was judicious. Even after two or three further visits to the country I could not raise any enthusiasm for this. One of my abiding recollections of Seoul is the sight of high rise apartments with each balcony crowded with jars of this nutritious but, to me, nauseous vegetable. During the meal I explained my sad predicament with regard to my missing luggage, and worse still my total lack of financial independence. Immediately they put my fears to naught. They would regularly telephone the airport to check on the arrival of my baggage, and better still they would take me shopping in the afternoon to complete my wardrobe. This proved to be harder than I had imagined. The average size of the Korean man was considerably less then even my not too tall frame. I managed to obtain some shirts and underclothes, which if I held my breath would do until my own clothes arrived.

There remained two outstanding areas which I had to deal with. The following year we were to have a dress rehearsal for the main event. The Asian Games were to be held in Seoul and would run the three disciplines in a similar manner to the real thing, except that the cross-country course would be considerably smaller to cope with the less experienced horses. Teams were to come from Hong Kong, Indonesia, India and other countries of the Pacific rim. The African countries were excluded because of the risk of African Horsesickness, which is endemic in that area. One team was due from Kuwait, which was by then accepted by the authorities as free from all the nasty equine diseases. The arrival of the horses from abroad would entail a few days quarantine before the animals were allowed onto the competition site. In order to progress this I had to ensure that the quarantine stables were adequate and comfortable for the incoming horses. I was taken out to the two chosen sites, one of which would require considerable alteration to ensure the safety of the incumbents. Various small matters such as door locks which could catch a horse's eye when led in and out of the stable, and window frames which could easily be broken by an inquisitive nose, had to be seen to. My colleagues assured me that all these would be seen to before next year.

The other pressing problem concerned the feed and bedding which would be available for the horses. When I inquired I was told that this was no worry as they had plenty of rice straw for bedding and sufficient amounts of home-made hay. For concentrates there was good barley. Looking at the hay, I realised that Korea was not a prime grass growing country. The sample offered to me was dry and dusty and certainly not to be greeted with acclamation by teams from abroad, used to high quality racehorse hay. I knew that some countries abhorred hay made from Timothy grass, and others desired a good mixture of clover or lucerne hay. The Australians fed oat straw in liberal quantities. There was nothing for it, but for me to go home and try to organise the import of the necessary items into Korea. This was an unexpected addition to my chores as the official veterinary surgeon. However I am pleased to say that I was able to buy large quantities of all the feedstuffs, as well as straw and shredded paper for bedding. I was asked by one competitor to ensure that an adequate supply of vacuum packed grass would also be in the stables. To my surprise this rider actually used none of the grass, but it was soon snapped up by other teams who had never seen such a product before.

As we returned to the main arena, I walked into an old acquaintance of mine, who was to be in charge of the air transport of the foreign teams. We suddenly realised that we should need to view the vehicles, which were destined to take the horses from the aeroplanes to the quarantine stables and thence on to the competition. We were shown three army trucks, which had been put aside for this purpose. I well knew that there would be some high jump specialist horses coming to the Games, but I doubted if they would feel like performing onto an open lorry immediately after a twelve hour flight around the globe. Equally, unless we were to build ramps at each destination, how were they to get off this novel form of horsebox? After at least three high-level talks, the organisers agreed that my colleague should order the necessary horse boxes to be built in England prior to the arrival of the animals next year.

One final problem struck me. As I assessed the emergency first aid facilities, I was shown a horse trailer attached to a four wheel drive vehicle. This was a routine trailer, with no capacity to pull a fallen horse into the recesses of the box. I was told that they were sure there would be plenty of help to pull on a rope. Remembering that television would be broadcast worldwide, I did not look forward to the sight of a group of helpers man-handling a stricken horse into the box. I suggested that some form of winch and wire pulley should be fixed to enable the transfer of a patient off the competition site and to the hospital. To my surprise this seemed to be beyond the powers of the local electricians, despite the fact that the country was by then one of the leaders in world electrical goods. I forthwith agreed that I would see what I could find in England.

After completing my survey of all the facilities, I took my leave of my excellent hosts, and caught a plane to Australia, still without any sign of my luggage. This was to arrive where I was staying in Sydney two days after my arrival there. It was with considerable relief that I greeted my possessions, fortunately as intact as when I had last seen them on the other side of the world. As I thought of my time in Seoul I wondered what I had forgotten to check? Would my suggestions find favour on second thoughts and actually be put into practice? I could only wait until my next visit and keep my fingers crossed. At least I was able to make contact with a dealer in Australia, who undertook to arrange for sufficient oats, wheat straw and oat straw to be sent by ship to Korea. The remainder of the feedstuffs I would obtain at home. On my return to Europe I was at least able to inform the FEI that the basic health conditions for the horses appeared to be quite adequate. The local laboratory in Seoul was to undertake the necessary tests on the horses to ensure their freedom from disease on arrival. From our previous experience in flying horses to Australia, I did not anticipate any problems from the long trip. This thankfully was borne out in practice. None of the animals for either Games arrived any the worse for their unaccustomed journeys.

Next year arrived with undue haste, as it frequently seems to do when one is apprehensive as to what it will bring. I returned to Seoul ten days before the first foreign horses were due to fly in. This time I was not alone. The official team appointed by the FEI met me at the hotel. The course builder for the Three Day Event was well known to me at home. The Technical Delegate, who was in charge of all the competition organisation, was a man from Canada, who proved to have a totally unflappable manner. This was to be a great asset to the rest of us in times of growing stress. The third member of the official team was an American lady, very experienced in all areas of competition administration. She was to find a disturbing degree of sex bias in the initial stages. The Koreans had an inborn dislike of taking orders and advice from a member of the fairer sex. Between us we began to view the preparations for the Games. I was pleased to see that most of my suggestions had been taken up, and things started to look hopeful. The food had arrived, and despite some grumbling at the cost, was generally approved. The transport was in order, and my Korean colleagues had received some instruction on the use of the hospital facilities.

I met with the third member of my Commission, a vet from the local National laboratory. As I spoke to him, I realised to my despair that although he was well qualified in his job, he had no experience whatsoever of the equine world. This was not good news, since I had already met the second member of my team, an Indian army vet, who was not over-inclined to exert himself in matters pertaining to the task in hand. He was apparently a person of some importance in the Asian Federation, and as such was to spend the majority of his time attending various parties and celebrations with his peers. It looked very much as though I was to be on my own throughout the ten days of competition. As it turned out the Korean vet could not have been more helpful and soon learned exactly what was required of him. Once we had accepted that we were not to have the full concentration of the Indian, we were happy to take him into what was to prove a congenial group.

The day before the first horses were due in, we were joined by the judges for the various events. Three were appointed by the FEI for their expertise in their particular discipline. They came from differing countries and backgrounds. A Danish shipping man, a lady law judge from Hong Kong and a landowner from France. They questioned us as to the preparations for their own individual competitions, and were told they must wait, nothing was certain until things got underway.

These started with the first inspection of the horses, the purpose of the inspection being to ensure that all the competitors were fit enough to start. Since there were only about fifty horses for the games in total, we tended to see a horse presented for more than one competition. One particular horse from Indonesia certainly came back for each discipline, being adjudged just all right to compete on each occasion. It was no bigger than a pony, and had a pony's short action, which made it difficult to know if it was truly sound. The Three Day Event went off without a hitch, although the standard was no higher than a novice class at home. It was won to great delight by a Korean rider, whose father immediately told me that his son could now win the Olympic title in two years time. I did not wish to disabuse him of this, but merely said that I hoped that he would be able to get some more tuition in the intervening period.

On the next day, before the start of the Show Jumping, I was struck down with an excruciating pain in my neck. I managed to survive the day on liberal doses of aspirin, but come evening the pain got worse. I had noticed a sign in the hotel, advertising massage in the basement. This seemed a good solution to my problem, so I descended the steps and booked in for a massage. Needless to say nobody there spoke one word of English, but I was shown into a consulting room, and lay down on the bed. I was shortly followed by a young lady, dressed in a leotard, whose first action was to dim the lights. Lying there in the gloom I watched her take off her shoes. Oh dear, had I made a great mistake? Never mind how beautiful she might be, I was in no state for party games. Without more ado she climbed up onto the table and proceeded to walk up and down my back. This did not seem to be the right approach to easing my pain, so I said that the problem area was in my neck. Since my words were jibberish to her, she continued her march with greater intensity. To bring this to a halt I sat up, nearly decanting her to the floor, and pointed to my neck with a grimace. The message got through, and she seized my head with gusto and began to try and twist it off my body. I leaped off the couch, thanked her for her valiant efforts, paid her the required sum, and crawled back up to the bar.

There I joined the judges who were enjoying an evening drink. Ordering a large Scotch, I sat back looking exhausted. My state intrigued the elderly Show Jumping judge, and he asked where I had been. Explaining that I had just had a massage from a scantily clad young Korean girl, he asked if it would be good for him. Nastily I suggested that he should definitely try it. With that he got up, prepared for a pre-dinner extravaganza. I am sorry to say that on his return he looked every year of his age. Looking at me malevolently, he vowed to get his own back before we went home. Thankfully he never had the chance. My saviour came in the form of the lady judge from Hong Kong. She told me that she had studied the history of Eastern massage and physiotherapy and offered to apply her knowledge to my neck. I don't know how fierce she became when wearing her wig in court, but she was the epitome of gentleness in her methods. There was no doubt that her healing touch soothed my aches. Finishing, she gave me a small plaster to put on my shoulder. This I was told would continue the cure, as it was impregnated with various herbs. Events proved that the cure was every bit as effective as I had been told.

The Asian Games continued on their way without providing the vets with any great problems. We did unfortunately lose one horse, which was found dead in its stable one morning. A post-mortem showed that it had suffered a massive heart attack. I took the opportunity to assemble my first aid team to remove the animal from the stable. It seemed a good idea to try out the horse ambulance, now fitted with the power winch and cable. Leaving them to carry on, I was hastily summoned back by one of the vets to come and help, as all did not seem to be going according to plan. They had attached the horse to the cable and proceeded to drive the vehicle forwards. Alas they had uncoupled the trailer and fixed the cable to the back of the Land Rover with the result that the ambulance was having a free ride, propelled by the horse. I showed them that the winch should be doing the pulling within the trailer and not the vehicle. After one hour we managed to evacuate the wretched animal. Not a promising start for a speedy exit from the show ring.

Korean Kerfuffle

During the dressage competition, ever eager to improve my knowledge, I heard two men sitting behind me discussing the various movements and the allotted scores. Turning round I said that as they appeared to know what was going on could they give me some hints. The elder of the two willingly fell in with my request, and explained in great detail what should have been done as opposed to what actually was taking place. When the competition was over, I thanked him for his help and congratulated him on his lucid explanations. Later that day I asked somebody who was the gentleman that seemed so knowledgeable about dressage. I was told to my eternal chagrin that he was the reigning World Champion dressage rider. No wonder he was so expert, but how kind to bother to keep my education up to scratch.

Once the whole competition was over the officials held a meeting with the Korean organisers. To everybody's alarm they began by saying what a success it had all been, and they were sure that they were now quite capable of running the big event at the Olympics itself. To my horror I thought again of the episode with the ambulance, and the misplaced optimism of the father of the winning Three Day Event rider. Surely when the main competitors arrived we should need more assistance. To my relief the remainder of our party quickly dispelled any feelings of self-congratulation, and it was agreed that some forty experienced people from Europe and America would come over to act as stewards, fence judges and general helpers. On the final evening, the head of the Korean Federation invited us all out to a celebratory dinner. I especially remember this as my pride in my new found ability to eat with chop sticks was found sadly wanting when presented with some special silver sticks with points like knitting needles. Defeated, I was forced to ask for a Western spoon and fork.

I retired home feeling that we would be able to cope with all the fates might throw at us. Accompanied by my two experienced surgeons

I should feel much happier. One last request I made to the organisers was that I should be provided with some form of transport during the Games. The arena was some half a mile from the stable complex and the hospital. This may not sound much, but when you were to make the journey at least two dozen times a day, it would prove a great boon.

The next year I once again visited Korea with the whole party of the FEI officials to ensure that everything would be ready for the big day. Apart from some worries as to the efficiency of the first aid parties, my side of the affairs caused no particular problems. I did decide that since the cross-country site was so far from the stables it would be necessary for the competitors to journey up the day before. Accordingly I checked that the stables there were adequate for two nights stay, and more importantly that there was accommodation for the riders and grooms and for two of the vets. The one thing that I forgot was to organise any food for myself and my colleague. This did not occur to me until the actual day arrived and everybody went off to supper.

At last it was time to follow the now familiar route back to Korea. I had never been to any Olympics before, so I did not know what to expect. The first surprise was the reception at the airport in Seoul. Those of us who were to act in any official capacity were whisked through the formalities and driven off to our hotels with welcoming greetings.

I had arrived some two and a half weeks before the first competition in order to conduct a final check that everything was ready. The other FEI officials met me at the hotel, and we sat down to consider what would undoubtedly go wrong. Pessimism is the lot of anybody trying to organise a group of fussy competitors and even more so their delicate mounts. Our party was increased by a splendid American lady, who was to be in charge of the stables. Known to all as Susan Stables, she was a tower of strength, and better still imbued with a great sense of humour. This was to prove invaluable to me as the continuing stream of questions and complaints rained in to my office. This office proved to be a magnet for all. It was only after some time that I realised that it was not my personal charm that drew people, but rather the fact that the office had the only outside telephone line in the complex.

Having made sure that all the feed and bedding was present and in good order, I had to allocate the various stable blocks to each country. It was important that each country was placed close to other countries from the same world area in order to minimise any possible disease problem. For example the Europeans, who anyway were in the main to share an aeroplane, could share a unit. The horses from South America had to be separated, as had those from Japan, since at that time diseases such as Japanese Encephalitis, and Venezuelan Equine Encephalitis were not unknown in those respective lands. The necessary quarantine stables had been prepared, and there was one unit on the racecourse site, well separated from the other stables. This would be used by the incoming horses from Europe. The surface of the lungeing rings and other exercise areas were walked over to make sure that no stones or other obstacles would injure the dainty feet of the horses. The actual competition site was looked after by an official 'footing expert', who produced an excellent surface of which not one person complained.

One source of worry was the site for the horse inspections. We had previously agreed that this should be in front of the stands so that the audience could have a good view of the horses. Unfortunately the surface proved unsuitable, being too soft to enable the Jury to identify any lameness. I had the bright idea that we should instead use the parade ring of the racecourse at the back of the stands. This had been newly laid down with a rubber surface that seemed to be eminently safe for the horses to trot over. Unfortunately it was not such a good idea in practice, since the rubber surface stopped the animals' hind feet sliding forward after hitting the ground. This resulted in a peculiar action, which made several of the horses look lame in a hind leg. However despite this, the initial inspections really caused no trouble. The final and most important inspection of the Three Day Event was to be held at the cross-country site, so we could dispense with the rubber problem.

I managed to cadge a lift up to the cross-country area with the course builder and spent a happy morning mooching around the jumps, most of which looked terrifying to me, but in fact were so well built that they caused surprisingly little worry for the riders. My morning stroll was rudely interrupted when a cloud of pamphlets came down like snow from the heavens. Picking one up, I saw that it was written in English, and emanated from North Korea, which was no distance from the course. It promised mayhem and disaster if the Games were permitted to begin. Fortunately nobody seemed to take this seriously and in the event nothing untoward happened but nevertheless it did little for my morale that morning.

The time came for the arrival of the first horses from abroad, and I went to the airport to see how they had travelled. To my relief they all stepped onto the tarmac as if they had only been on an hour's jaunt. Having seen them arrive, I rushed ahead to the stables to see them into their quarantine premises. I discovered that none of the stables had been bedded down. I asked for volunteers to get the thirty odd boxes ready for the arrivals. To my annoyance my pleas fell on deaf ears. With that I seized a fork and began to start on the boxes, aided only by my two surgeons. One of these was a professor at an esteemed veterinary school in Australia and the other a world renowned abdominal surgeon from the USA. I doubt if anyone of the three of us had grabbed a pitch fork in anger for many years, but it gradually shamed some of the onlookers into coming to join us. I am afraid that I lost considerable credence with the locals for undertaking such a menial task. One of the

Korean officials took me on one side and implied that I had somehow let officialdom down and demeaned my official uniform. As this took the form of a particularly nasty salmon pink coloured blazer, I did not feel over-sorry for my actions.

Once the horses were installed in the stables, the Korean Ministry of Agriculture took charge to make sure that all the health papers were correct. This brought about a major international incident when one horse from Venezuela came in with the horses from the USA. It had flown in direct from South America to join the flight from USA to Korea. Under the current health rules it should not have been with those horses at all, and the Koreans wanted it sent straight back from where it had come. Needless to say the rider and his countrymen took great exception to this ruling. High-level talks began with various embassies in Seoul, and a meeting was called with all the vets and riders to try and resolve the issue. The chief problem was whether in view of this horse's presence in the stables, this would compromise the chances of all the other horses being accepted back into their home countries. It was suggested that the team vets should take the responsibility for such a decision, until we pointed out that was certainly not within their remit.

Finally the authorities were persuaded that the risk of the horse having Venezuelan Equine Encephalitis was so small as to be virtually negligible. They agreed that it could stay so long as it remained quarantined on its own throughout the time it would be in the country. This was managed, but caused a few problems. For a start it was a show jumper and the rider naturally wished to carry on some practice. As a result, one of the helpers from Europe could be seen struggling across the compound on several occasions, carrying differing components of jumps. In addition, when the jumping competition began, this horse had to come to the arena by a circuitous route to enter from the opposite end to everyone else. The rules of the Olympic Games specify that only those horses with the top results from the preliminary competitions can take part in the individual final. Since this final is held as the last event in the main athletic arena, bets were being taken as to whether this horse would qualify, and if so how he was to be admitted. Murphy's law being what it is, of course it did qualify. Many suggestions as to how not to break the quarantine restrictions were forthcoming, the most bizarre being that he could be flown into the arena by helicopter. In fact he was to travel in his own special fumigated lorry and had a stable prepared for him in solitary state under the stands.

This experience emphasised the importance of making absolutely sure that the rules were followed before arranging transport abroad. We had encountered a similar situation during the Asian Games, when the Korean Ministry would not accept that a blood test on the Indian horses was free from any indication of disease as certified by the authorities in Delhi. That worry was only sorted out by taking a further set of blood samples and sending them to the Ministry of Agriculture laboratory in England, who were able to confirm the Indian results to the satisfaction of the Koreans.

The Three Day Event proceeded as planned, leaving the Australian professor and myself to attempt to find something to eat on the night before the cross-country phase. One of the teams, who had had the foresight to send out for a copious quantity of sandwiches and wine had pity on us. Strictly speaking we were contravening the rules in that we sat in on the team conference and briefing for the next day during our meal. It was interesting to hear how they planned their approach to the different fences, and in truth had no effect on our judgement except to raise our admiration for their aplomb in tackling what to me looked impossible fences. We were amused by the noise from the next room, where another team was also engaged in a briefing. This operation was interspersed at regular intervals by the departure of yet another competitor in tears from their conference. Regrettably they were not to prosper on the morrow.

Security was a major facet of the Games. We were driven from our hotel to the site in a bus, escorted by motor cycle outriders, armed to the teeth. Following my meeting with the propaganda leaflets on the course, I was not as irritated by this scare as were some of the others in the bus. Security did momentarily go mad on our arrival at the cross-country stables, where the guards were initially only prepared to let the horses into the stable area, but no humans. After explaining to the officer in charge that some fifty loose horses might present them with further problems not necessarily connected with security, they reluctantly agreed to let the grooms accompany their charges.

My transport at the complex took the form of a moped, with which I was neither familiar nor particularly safe. On one occasion I jumped on the machine to return to the hospital, forgetting that I had previously chained and padlocked the front wheel to save it from other thieving hands. In front of an admiring group of bystanders I executed a spectacular somersault, landing firmly on my back. I refrained from responding to requests for an encore, and made my way back stiffly to my office. When I was about to return to the arena, my ever-trusting professor requested a lift on the pillion. This journey was unfortunately recorded for posterity on film, which was later produced in a leading British equine journal. I have to admit that I was amazed at the confidence which my passenger's face expressed. He obviously had not been aware of my recent acrobatics.

Apart from the final show jumping competition, the dressage completed the Games. It was a pleasure to watch such high class performances, and I was this time guided through the movements by Wendy's sister, who was in Korea as jumping advisor to the British pentathlon team. The Games proved to be a success for the German teams, who won all three disciplines. The only veterinary incident involved a horse which developed pleuro-pneumonia. It was at last a chance for my American friend to ply his skill. He was I am afraid, sorry not to have had more calls on his expertise. I was amused to go to the unfortunate animal's stable to see not only Jack, but also his wife, an equally qualified veterinary surgeon, listening intently to the horse's chest. Each was engaged in auscultating the lung sounds. This was surely the quickest recipe for divorce, since it is widely known that no two vets can ever agree over their findings, let alone husband and wife. Alas even their valiant efforts failed to save the horse, and it became our only casualty throughout the whole episode.

It was a most interesting and in many ways a gratifying experience which I would not have missed for anything. It had been continuing hard work, which absorbed so much of my time that I saw little or nothing of the remainder of the Olympics. I had hoped to get to see at least some of the athletic events, but only managed to visit on the final day of the relays. I was surprised to note that unlike on television, one had a job to identify the individual participants. The TV that was shown to us on the set in our office consisted of interminable re-runs of boxing or wrestling. Worse still I could not find the time to do any serious shopping, so that my arrival home to Wendy was not one of unmixed joy. I am sure that I need not have been so engrossed in the task, but I never felt that I could safely leave the responsibility in the hands of my fellows on the commission. Additionally by the time the Games were over I found that my hotel expenses amounted to a considerable sum, running into four figures. This was engendered by the hoteliers deciding to raise the room prices halfway through the time, which left the FEI facing a much larger bill than had been estimated.

Nothing could have been more different from my previous life, and it left some very happy memories. However after five weeks in Korea I was not too sorry to return home. It was to be my finale with the FEI since my term of office on the veterinary committee was already overdue. I can only hope that in future the Olympic organisation will choose countries with more experience of the events for which they are being asked to provide facilities.

CHAPTER 15

Launched into the Law (1980's/1990's)

When I was seventeen years old, possessed of several Higher Certificate grades in classics, I was destined to read law at Oxford. The war was ending and my thoughts were heading to the aftermath. I consulted my housemaster as to which college I should apply. He recommended Trinity, based on the fact that it had the best cellar in the university. I duly wrote an application to the Master and was accepted for the term beginning in eighteen months time. Not as difficult as it is today!

Suddenly in the summer holiday I had a Damascan revelation. The thought of years cooped up in offices, coupled with the fact that I was living in a horse racing area, decided me to change course dramatically and follow a veterinary career. Now, since the veterinary calling is one of the scientific professions, this necessitated a massive re-think in my scholastic work. The school were more than accommodating, despite ardent attempts to turn my thoughts to human medicine. They transferred me to the areas of chemistry, physics and biology. This was of course totally foreign to me. Although I could fathom some of the intricacies of biology, chemistry and physics were foreign languages. To be truthful they still are; I can no more understand the workings of the telephone than I can fathom the more complicated betting patterns of racing punters.

Despite all of the problems I spent a happy year sitting in the rear of classes admiring the knowledge of my colleagues, most of whom were at least two years my junior. When the time came I managed to confuse the examiners to the extent that they gave me sufficiently good Higher levels to gain entry to the Royal Veterinary College. Once again a letter to the Principal announcing my desire to attend the next course sufficed to start me on a new career. No small wonder that present day undergraduates look on my generation as the spoiled ones.

Fortunately I practised in a non-litigious age. The practice were members of an organisation called the Veterinary Defence Society, although apart from signing a small cheque to them every year I never gave them a thought until I had been working for twenty odd years. I was suddenly accused by a retired bookmaker of failing to diagnose that his mare was in foal, thus losing him the chance to make a fortune at the horse sales in December. I asked the office staff if we were still insured against such outrageous slanders on my professional acuity. Learning that we were covered for such claims of professional negligence, I telephoned the consultant named on the policy. He came down to see me and said he would happily write a cheque there and then to pay for the claimed damages. I remonstrated with him that there was no evidence at that time that I was wrong, except the reported word of a vet, who had examined the mare and said she was indeed in foal. We decided to await the arrival of the disputed foal. The time went by when she was due, but no foal! The claims consultant phoned me, laughing, and said that I would be amused to learn that he had received a claim against the second vet by my bookmaker acquaintance for saying the mare was in foal when she clearly had not been.

This story illustrates the casual and happy state of the Society at that time. It was no more than a cottage industry run by a few vets for those in the profession who wished to take part. It was in 1982, after I had left practice, when a colleague of my college days asked if I would act as an expert witness in a large case concerning some brood mares. Since this was my main area of expertise, and since the lure of the legal life had never been entirely dissipated, I agreed to see if I could help. I met my colleague and a representative of a big legal firm in London for what was to be the first of many case conferences. Since the claim revolved around an infectious disease, I read up all the references to refresh my memory. I well remembered one of my partners having a dispiriting experience in the witness box of the High Court many years before. His case concerned an alleged poisoning of some horse with strychnine. Sorry to tell, the defending QC had read more about the effects of this drug in horses than had my partner. The result was an embarrassing hour in the witness box and the dismissal of what had seemed a cut and dried case.

The first lesson at the case conference was I suppose an obvious one, every word became important and was studiously taken down in long hand by the legal representative. Not for him the rough notes which I had been used to. We ran through the details of the claim and I tried to put the salient points in perspective. Since my presence was partly to give my own expert opinion, but also to suggest supporting witnesses to strengthen the case for the defence, I decided that as the claim was sizable we would require an acknowledged expert in this particular disease. I knew a friendly professor in the States, who had devoted his life to the study of this area of veterinary knowledge, so I agreed to enlist his help. The professor readily agreed to come to London to lend his expertise to us. He was a big man, an Irish American with determined ideas. He brooked no doubt when confronted with the details of the claim. He assured the barrister and his junior at our next meeting that the opposition had no grounds for complaint, since the basis of their case was scientifically unsound. The whole situation put on a more rosy appearance. I had but one doubt, which I expressed to the counsel. To my surprise he straightaway said that he would not wish for me to go into the witness box, lest I sink his argument. This was initially a disappointment to me, as I was looking forward to my chance to show off my debating skills against the opposing counsel, whom incidentally I had known personally for some years.

After several more visits to the solicitor's office, the day arrived for the trial. We all arrived in The Strand in our best town suits with shoes well polished and the case bundles carefully held under our arms. At least we were not going to let the judge think we did not appreciate the gravity of his court. At first sight the court room was awesome. Rows of uncomfortable wooden benches for the participants, the foremost being kitted out with water jugs and glasses to relieve the drying throats of the leading counsel, who were alone allowed to address the judge. Of the latter there was no sign as we settled into our seats. The two opposing sides cast inquisitive glances at each other, trying to assess who was who and which members of the press were present at the rear. The court clerk drifted in and out looking like a crow, who could not decide on its perch for the night. After a few minutes he glided in his cloak through a door at the side of the room. Returning, he demanded that the audience all stand to welcome the judge, dressed in his magisterial robes. He bowed to those in the court, and we all bowed back as he took his seat. One felt that he should have been provided with an orchestra to conduct or at the very least a grand piano on which to perform.

The proceedings began by the chief advocates introducing themselves to the judge. The opposition's counsel then laid out the details of the claim, giving a very comprehensive explanation of the losses his client claimed to have suffered, and continued to explain why the defendants were at fault. Although I knew him to be an excellent horseman himself I was impressed at his knowledge of the veterinary elements in dispute. The first witness was the lady who was, she felt, the injured party. Her place in the witness box was taken by her expert, who went into great detail about the scientific principles. Many of his arguments I considered misplaced, and I was urged by the solicitor to note my comments and pass them over the row to our barrister. All the time the solicitor was busy writing every word down, as indeed it seemed did the judge. No concession to the modern world such as tape recorders. I was sure that if an eighteenth century lawyer had walked into the room he would have felt immediately at home. In fact I was sorry to see that quill pens were no longer in evidence.

At the end of the first day, which finished at the early hour of four o'clock, despite the start only taking place at eleven o'clock, we retired somewhat dispirited since the case against us had been well presented. We awoke next morning to scan the papers. The racing journals had reported the opposition's case in detail, which did little for our morale. I was to learn that this was common practice, the public's interest being thought to have a span of only twenty four hours. As a result there was no mention on subsequent days of our defence.

The arguments continued at a snail's pace over the next three days. I was rapidly coming to the conclusion that I had chosen a profession more in tune with my impatient nature. At long last our counsel got up to present a contrary point of view. His previous cross examination of the witnesses had exposed some deficiencies, on which he now proceeded to elaborate. My professor was sworn in, and I felt that we had reached the denouement of the prosecution's chances. All went according to plan until the other counsel started his cross-examination. He posed a number of innocent questions and then quietly suggested that his own expert had taken a different view. Could this not be a possible explanation of the problems? To my dismay the American expert became rattled and lost his bluster, agreeing that perhaps an alternative theory could have been right. Not for the last time I discovered that the majesty and formality of a court room could deflate even the most adamant of witnesses.

We adjourned to lick our wounds. This was where our counsel astonished me by his sure grasp of his brief. He cheerfully said that the veterinary evidence was not the most telling and we should await events. On returning to court he asked the judge if he could call the plaintiff's accountant. Quick whispering in the corner of the court brought the agreement that they would produce the accountant after the week-end. We congregated once more on the Monday in eager, if confused anticipation. Further hastily organised discussions between the barristers took place in the lobby, resulting in a favourable settlement for our defendants and the case suddenly came to a conclusion.

Despite my reading of the importance of the veterinary evidence, our astute counsel had seen from the beginning that the opposition's Achilles heel lay in matters of non-disclosure of tax and a failure of accurate book keeping. No wonder they had capitulated so quickly. The moral for me was that the obvious was not always the most important facet. My admiration for the legal profession rose very considerably. I learned from our counsel that his next brief concerned an argument over the minutiae of ship building. I am sure that he would once more sound as though he had spent his life on the Clyde, just as he had made us believe that his past months had been passed on a thoroughbred stud.

I gained a great deal from my baptism into the legal life, which was to prove of great benefit in years to come. Firstly I understood the etiquette of the courts, which can be terrifying on first acquaintance. Secondly I realised that the trained legal mind can see further through a tangled web of conflicting stories than is apparent to a layman. Thirdly and most importantly I discovered that the most confident witness can be reduced to jelly when confronted by an astute prosecutor. As I was to learn in time, the High Court bore only a passing resemblance to that which transpired in the lower echelons of the law. Once one enters the County Courts, justice may become something like a lottery. Judges there may appear to dismiss the spoken word, preferring to make up their own minds on the veracity of the various witnesses. They will fall over backwards in many cases to offer aid and sympathy to the plaintiff without legal support.

My part in this case had been very interesting and relaxed. My colleague was responsible to the Veterinary Defence Society for the possible ultimate costs, and his worries multiplied through the early days of the procedure. Fortunately his frequent discussions with the Society's reinsurers at Lloyds were harmonious and he was given whole-hearted backing throughout. After the dust had settled he invited me to a Council meeting of the Society to give my views on the case. There it was suggested that I might like to join their team of claims consultants. My interest in the law had certainly been re-kindled and this looked like being an ideal combination in which to pursue my learning curve.

The claims group at that time consisted of four experienced vets, all of whom had spent their professional lives in practice. As the claims arrived from those unfortunate members who had fallen foul of one of their clients it was the task of the consultant to decide firstly on the rightness of the claim, and then to either make a settlement or to take up the cudgels on behalf of the member. The motto of the Society was impressed on me - Defence and not Defiance.

At that time the Society was dealing with around three hundred claims a year, a figure that was to grow in my time to just under one thousand. Such was the growth of the litigious age. I was indeed glad that I had practised in happier times. Very soon I was allotted one or two simple cases to deal with. At the beginning these might refer to any species, a situation that was gradually to alter as the numbers rose and I became solely involved with equines.

One of my first cases concerned the sad tale of a lady who had brought her little dog into the surgery. She had asked the dizzy receptionist if the vet could remove its talons. The girl mistook her request for "talents" instead of "talons". No doubt her teenage mind was more concerned with sex than toe nails. At any rate the vet rendered the poor male dog infertile and returned the emasculated hound to its owner, who was naturally not best pleased with the outcome. She consulted her solicitor with a view to receiving compensation. Needless to say, this mongrel-bred creature had a great stud career in front of it, despite then being ten years of age with no noticeable planned progeny. My discussions with the poor solicitor to reduce the amount of the claim to more reasonable proportions was lengthy. Finally I received a phone call from him to request some form of settlement as his lady staff were ribbing him and implying that he would not have wished such an operation. I agreed on a suitable settlement, but fifteen years have gone by and the Society has heard no more from him nor his client.

Shortly I was to embark on my first complicated equine claim. For this I enlisted the help of one of the Society's lawyers, a lovely man who was tragically to die from cancer within a very few years at a ludicrously young age. The case continued for some months and then went mysteriously quiet for some four years. It was eventually resuscitated not to our surprise, since we felt that the client was indeed due some recompense. The final settlement beat all outstanding records for the Society, being in the region of a quarter of a million pounds. This did not seem a promising start to my career.

Visits to the courts of the British Isles were thankfully rare, averaging around two or three a year. My first visit was to Worksop County Court to discuss a claim over the height of a jumping pony. Together with our legal advisor from Liverpool and a promising barrister, now an eminent QC, we met up at a hotel the night before to interview our member once more. In the morning our happy party made for the court. We had all heard a great deal about the national miners' strike at that time, but it was with considerable surprise and some hesitation that we passed through several road blocks crammed with the constabulary. Parking the car close to the court, my confederates went on ahead to obtain a consulting room. I wandered on behind, turned left under an archway and climbed some stairs to find myself in the headquarters of the miners' strike committee. Tentatively I asked if they knew where the court house was. Laughter greeted me, accompanied by recognition of The Sporting Life which I had under my arm. It was obvious that at least five of the seven or eight were confirmed racing enthusiasts. Asking where I was from and learning that I came from near Lambourn, I was besieged by requests for tips for that day's racing at Lingfield. I reluctantly recommended a horse in the four o'clock race, hoping that by that time I would have made my escape. As it turned out I increased the strike fund by varying amounts at five to one. One of the men volunteered to guide me to the court. Following him I was alarmed to see a posse of police in the entrance to the court. Suspecting at least some verbal abuse, I sidled past my guide, only to hear him greeting one of the force cheerily by christian name.

"Do we expect any trouble here today, Bill?" asked the copper.

"Not today, old boy. The main troops are further south and have been told to stay away from here," responded my guide. So much for the bitter struggle always portrayed in the media.

I joined my team in the consulting room, and suggested that since the argument related to the pony being possibly an inch over the required height, our member should remove one shoe in the witness box to emphasise the difference that the shoes on a pony can make. This was greeted with horror by our barrister. He thought that the judge would feel his court was being made into a music hall by such a comic demonstration. As events turned out such a show was not necessary, since after several clandestine meetings between the two advocates, the other side withdrew their complaint and we retired homewards with honour satisfied. This was but one of the claims which were withdrawn at the court door, costing the Society much time, aggravation and money.

During my years with the VDS I travelled to many and varied courts of the British Isles. The courts ranged from modern purpose built buildings to those which Mr Pickwick himself would have recognised. Many were so designed as to make hearing the participants virtually impossible. The temperature could be icy cold or so hot as to encourage the majority of the players to nod off.

One particular claim in Ireland was heard in a room which resembled a Dublin bar rather than an august place of justice. The gentleman in charge had the look of an Irish pixie. He was of such small stature that he could scarcely see over his desk. Our appointed time for the start was 10.30am, but what with numerous matrimonial disputes, debt arguments and other small legal matters we did not begin the hearing until quarter past twelve. Half an hour later the judge intimated that he was hungry and would be back again at quarter past two. On reassembling, the court was packed with lawyers and interested spectators. This was a claim about a horse, and to the Irish that proved irresistible. Our own advocate eventually found a seat from where he had some small chance of catching the judge's eye. The dispute this time concerned the suitability of our member's operating theatre. The plaintiff's case was supported solely by a building engineer, who in cross-examination admitted that until the previous day he had never seen an equine hospital. With that the claim looked considerably more shaky. Further argument ranged over the value of the unfortunate horse, which the plaintiff claimed would have been more than likely to win a Grand National and several other high class races. Our expert on valuation had done his homework and showed that the animal's form to that date was two starts in races, one finishing last in a point-to-point and the other pulled up when second last in another. It then became clear that our judge had made good use of his diminished stature by riding in a number of races himself. He asked some pertinent questions of the plaintiff and ended by remarking that he did not believe that he himself would have been too keen to purchase such a horse.

After the hearing concluded we were told that the judge would think about his verdict and give his finding when he next came to that particular court in two months time. Our solicitor was confident of the final result, but by the time we actually received notification that we had won, the plaintiff had done the proverbial runner and we were left with little or no chance of recovering our costs. It seemed that the horse was owned by a partnership of a number of men, who included a local publican, a roadsweeper, a milkman, and an unemployed labourer. Such frustrations were in no way limited to the Emerald Isle as both I and my colleagues had a long list of such pointless exercises.

Just as courts differed so do judges. I had the great misfortune one time to pursue an argument over a horse's foot in the County Court. Barristers often have a knowledge of horses from their time at the Inns of Court, where they actively pursued the pastime of riding, especially risking their necks in one of the races at the Bar point-to-point. In this instance the opposing counsel was well briefed on matters of farriery and soundness in general. He launched off into a detailed diatribe on the former. The judge suddenly intervened, saying he should declare an interest. Not only was he one of Her Majesty's respected guardians of justice, but also a fully qualified farrier. How unlucky can you get? He must have been the sole judge in the United Kingdom who combined two such disparate callings. Not surprisingly this was one day that we crept out of the court with our tails between our legs.

During my thirteen or so years as a claims consultant I listened with admiration to my colleagues discussing their own cases. Having spent my entire professional career in the world of horses, I knew virtually nothing about the small animal kingdom. Indeed one of the first things my wife realised about me on our marriage was that I could not be trusted to treat our own dogs. Shortly after our return from honeymoon one of our two dogs became sick, and without a thought Wendy took it off to the local opposition in the nearby town. I was happily on very good terms with this particular vet, so I was delighted with the arrangement.

The great buzz word in the professions today is rightly Continuing Professional Development, which simply means keeping up-to-date with modern advances in science. I can fully recommend a few sessions with the claims group for this purpose. I became passably knowledgeable about the intricacies of bloat in greyhounds and cruciate ligament repair in small dogs. However I was more than a little depressed by the frequency with which clients would rush to law over believed grievances. These were too often fuelled by second opinion practitioners, who seemed anxious to get one over on their neighbours. Sadly we knew to our cost that within the space of a few weeks they too would be seeking our help when the boot had transferred to the other foot.

Legal Aid was something that I had misguidedly believed existed to help the needy to bring to the courts some blinding injustice over houses or faulty advice from financial advisors. I had not realised that a girl purchasing a prospective Three Day Event horse for several thousand pounds could qualify for such assistance. This frequently made a drain on the Society's funds where the claim was totally spurious, since even when defeating the claim in court, we could obtain no contribution to our justifiable costs. Hopefully the legal authorities will begin to look more closely before they willingly offer support for such trivial and ill-thought claims.

One of my most frequent claims related to the purchase of a horse, which on arrival at its new home was said to be unfit for the purpose on which it had been bought. Sometimes this was due to an ailment missed by the examining vet, but much more commonly grievance was due to the purchaser being unable to ride the animal. Looking for a quiet hack, the purchaser would buy a racehorse straight from training and then be amazed that it was far too lively for them to sit on. For this reason we often decided that it was cheaper and quicker to buy the horse from them and sell it on to a home, which was more suitable. At one time the Society was the proud if reluctant owner of five horses and a cow. Happily all were satisfactorily found contented homes.

In my period with the VDS our solicitor team changed, initially as mentioned due to the sad death of our chief advisor. We were guided in later years by two charming ladies with whom it was a great pleasure to be associated. My admiration for their grasp of some of our esoteric problems grew as the years went by. Even more so did my wonder at their determination not to be outgunned by some of our opposing lawyers. One lady earned herself the kindly nickname of the Rottweiler for her persistence in demanding answers to her awkward questions. Court cases were made more enjoyable in their company, especially as their office always contained a recent addition of the Good Food Guide, which led us to many fine dinners between sessions in court.

The worst aspect of the law to me was the interminable length to which claimants could go to delay a final hearing of a claim. If anything my Irish friends had turned this into a fine art. One claim in particular lasted for ten years and still had not reached a conclusion when I ended my connection with the Society. By the time, if ever, it comes to court the animals concerned will be past history, and none of the participants will be able to summon a clear memory of the events in question.

My lasting impressions of my thirteen years with the Society were of a happy and interesting conclusion to my professional life. The companionship of the group made what could have been a depressing and stressful job a pleasurable experience. I must admit to lowering the tone of some of our discussions by a series of semi-facetious comments, but these were taken in good part by our chairman, whom I had known since college days and had since been honoured to be the best man at his wedding. The persistent complaints from some plaintiffs became at times very wearing, although I knew that their frequent letters and telephone calls were usually in reverse ratio to the validity of their claims. The members of the Society were well served by the team in the claims. Each consultant had at some time held office in one of the divisions of the British Veterinary Association, our equivalent of the BMA, and their combined knowledge was encyclopedic. Towards the end of my time one of my colleagues took to writing faxes to me in Greek which seemed to complete the full circle. This confirmed my conclusion that it was a good time to draw a line under my veterinary life; the lawyers had missed little by my choice of profession, but learning a little about their often peculiar systems had proved well worthwhile.

Finale

Looking back on nearly fifty years as a veterinary surgeon, I ask myself if I had indeed chosen a wise way of life. Satisfying, often frustrating, but active and healthy. It has been a life of continuing variations, with a number of highs and fortunately a fewer number of lows.

In these days of understandable and laudable worries about animal welfare, the veterinary surgeon must be in the forefront of those concerned with the health and contentment of our fellow creatures. Constant contact with them does not necessarily lead to the unfortunate anthropomorphism so mistakenly adopted by those of the militant animal rights groups. Unless you have a close attachment to your patients, you could not survive very long in the work. Certainly we often have to take an apparently hard-hearted approach, but this is tempered by consideration of the alternatives. To continue the life of a patient without regard to its future ability to enjoy a reasonable standard of life is an entirely misplaced judgement.

One of the obvious changes with regard to horses is the loss of owners with a lifelong connection with them. In the fifties there were still a number of people who had grown up in an age where the horse was the standard means of transport. As a result the husbandry was based on many years of experience. Today, despite the plethora of literature on up-to-date methods of keeping horses, the amateur still has little practical experience, which results in increasing demands on the veterinary profession and such bodies as the British Horse Society to give guidance. It is certainly true to say that the competition horse is better cared for than was the case in my earlier days, when the influence of the cavalry teaching had declined in the face of mechanisation.

Without a doubt if I was starting again I would choose the same course of life and can confidently recommend it to anyone with an abiding interest in all animals. As the farm animal falls prey to the need